TREES

BENJAMIN PERKINS

Grange

The Horse Chestnut in autumn.

CONTENTS

ACKNOWLEDGEMENTS

The author and Savitri Books wish to
express their grateful thanks to the
following, for their kindness and patience
in loaning paintings in their possession
for use in this book:

Mr. David Hart
Mr. and Mrs. Anthony Carlisle
Miss Penelope Stirling
Mr. and Mrs. R. M. Cullen
Mrs. Anne Dewe
Dr. S. Srivastava

Published by Grange Books
AN IMPRINT OF BOOKS & TOYS LTD
The Grange
Grange Yard
London SE1 3AG
England

ISBN 1 85627 051 3

© Benjamin Perkins (pictures & text), 1984
© Savitri Books Ltd (this edition and design), 1984, renewed 1991

This edition, 1991, is produced for Grange Books
by Savitri Books Ltd
Southbank House
Suite 106
Black Prince Road
London SE1 7SJ

Printed and bound in Hong Kong
Produced by Mandarin Offset Ltd

Stag beetle (Lucanus cervus).

BUCKINGHAM PALACE.

   The woods and trees are easily taken for granted as
a permanent feature of our landscape. Yet they are very
much a part of the whole complicated and interacting web
of life. Seen as part of the landscape they may look alike
but, as this book so beautifully illustrates, they belong
to a wide variety of species, some with a life-span longer
than others but all depending on and contributing to both
the immediate as well as the wider natural environment.

   The trouble is that the very environment on which they
depend is undergoing rapid and serious degradation. Diseases
are spreading from one continent to another and finding victims
lacking in genetic resistance; the insidious attack by air
pollution, sometimes known as acid rain, is becoming daily more
serious; the expansion of human habitation; industries and
agriculture are constantly eroding the areas left for trees
and woods. These threats can be mitigated but it will need
much greater understanding by Governments, more generous
consideration by developers, considerable funds and widespread
popular support.

   In this book, Benjamin Perkins makes a powerful case for
the conservation of one of the most familiar features of the
landscape.

1984

INTRODUCTION

*B*ack in 1968, I decided that I would like to undertake a series of drawings on some natural history subject, with an eventual book in mind, and started to cast about for a suitable theme. Birds, wild flowers, butterflies and moths – all subjects that had long interested me – had each been covered by numerous books, but it occurred to me that there had never been any really adequate illustrated work on trees. Since then, a number of books, of varying quality, have been published on this subject, but the best of these have had too wide a scope for all the stages of growth of each species to be illustrated, and many of the others contain irritating omissions or inaccuracies. My main reason for choosing the broad-leaved trees was that nearly every species native to, or naturalised in, Britain could, with a little trouble, be found within a few miles of my North Essex home. Furthermore, in seeking out some of the less common species by enquiry around the neighbourhood, the need for such a book became more and more apparent: even among country people it was surprising to discover how few tree species were readily recognised. Almost everyone was familiar with Oak, Ash and Elm, and most were able to identify a longer list of the commoner species; yet many people were unaware that there was more than one species of Oak or of Elm, and very few knew of such retiring species as the Black Poplar or the Wild Service Tree, although these trees were native to the district.

I therefore started work, in the summer of that year, on the colour plates; the object being to show all the stages of the tree's growth from dormant winter twig, through swelling bud and bud-burst, full leaf, flower and fruit, to the autumn leaf. Not all these stages were necessarily relevant to every species as potential aids to identifying the tree, but I tried to omit none which could assist recognition at any time of the year, bearing in mind particularly that early spring, when winter buds are swelling and breaking open to expose tufts of young leaves, can be a confusing period.

The black and white drawings show typical silhouettes of the deciduous species in winter (the four evergreen species, Holly, Box, Holm Oak and Strawberry Tree always being readily recognisable by their leaves), for although there is considerable variation in the shapes of individual trees, it is surprising how often, with a little practice, one can make a correct identification of a tree, even at quite a distance, from the outline alone. Each drawing is a portrait of an individual tree, and in the majority of cases it is the tree which provided the specimens for the corresponding colour plate. I have tried to choose mature trees with a typical configuration and to show not only the habit of trunk and main branches, but also to give some idea of the disposition and special characteristics of the smaller branches and twigs, which can be equally important. Thus the combination of branches curving down towards the ground and thick twigs curving upwards at their tips to give a 'shepherd's crook' effect, can make the Ash tree easily identifiable long before one has come close enough to observe the grey colour of the twigs or the sooty black buds; and a grove of Birches can be recognised as *B. pendula* rather than *B. pubescens* merely by observing their pendulous shoots. However, these characteristics provide only a guide and, particularly in the case of young trees or very old trees which have lost many of their branches, a closer inspection will often be necessary. The Birches, just mentioned, provide a case in point, since young trees of both species are narrow and spire-shaped, with upswept branches, and it is only as it gets older that the Silver Birch takes on its pendulous habit. Soil, aspect and altitude can also alter the appearance of trees, making them windswept, stunted or otherwise untypical; and trees growing in forests, where competition with neighbours draws them up beyond their normal height and robs them of their side branches, are frequently very different in shape from their open-grown cousins. For instance, the forest-grown Beech, instead of exhibiting a huge domed and spreading crown, may have fifty feet or more of straight, clean bole before the first branch. It is worth mentioning, incidentally, that identification, if there is any choice in the matter, should always be made from mature trees, and from twigs growing on one of the main branches, rather than from very vigorous young growth or from sucker or epicormic shoots, all of which are liable

Sweet Violet (*Viola odorata*).

to show untypical characteristics.

The criterion by which I have decided which species to include and which to exclude, has been whether or not one would be likely to come across them while walking in the country, anywhere in the British Isles. So I have excluded trees that one would only expect to find growing in parks, gardens, commercial plantations, arboreta, etc., but have included planted trees as well as wild-grown trees, and introduced as well as native species. For example, I have included the Locust Tree, a North American introduction, which I have frequently encountered in the woodland of East Anglia, where it readily spreads by means of root-suckers, but have left out such familiar garden species as the Tulip Tree or the Magnolias. Perhaps one exception to this rule is the Plane, which may never penetrate deeper into the rural scene than the park of some great mansion, and is most familiar as a town tree. Nevertheless, it appears in the book because, by reason of being so widely planted – in cities and country towns alike – it is one of the best known of all species, and therefore occupies a unique place among British trees.

Another criterion in selecting species was whether it truly qualified as a tree. My dictionary defines a tree as a 'perennial plant with single woody stem or trunk usually unbranched for some distance above ground'. It soon became apparent, however, that there were a number of species that hovered uncertainly upon the border line of trees on the one hand and shrubs and bushes on the other. The Holly is undoubtedly a tree, but what of the Hazel ? So often it is coppiced or continually cut down to hedge height, yet when left alone, it will grow to a height of twenty to thirty feet – sometimes over fifty feet in woodland – with sturdy, thick, albeit generally multiple, trunks. It is such an important and familiar constituent of the woodland that I decided to give it the benefit of the doubt, and the same applied to the Sallow or 'Pussy Willow'. Other species, however, which sometimes form small trees, but are much better known in the guise of shrubs, such as Spindle, Blackthorn and the Buckthorns, Elder and Osier, had to be omitted.

I have limited myself to broad-leaved trees because conifers would require an entirely different set of criteria. With only three native species – Scots Pine, Yew and Juniper – the numerous introduced species encountered outside gardens, parks, collections, etc. tend to be grown commercially and to be found chiefly in forestry plantations.

Work on the colour plates has taken a long time – some fifteen years – partly because of my farming commitments, such urgent activities as lambing, haymaking and harvest tending to coincide with all too brief stages in the tree's annual cycle of growth, and partly because such vital events as bud-burst and flowering often occur simultaneously on many different trees, so that only a small number of species could be dealt with in any one year. Sometimes good examples from which to make drawings were not available locally, and I had to seek them further afield – always with the chance of arriving too early or too late – and sometimes late frosts, drought, the depredations of insects or other natural disasters would force me to postpone a particular drawing to a subsequent year. On the whole, however, I was lucky in that the great majority of species could be found without having to travel very far, although it was sometimes easier to find a tree providing suitable specimens for the watercolours than a mature, open-grown and typical example of the same species for illustrating the whole tree in winter.

Primrose (*Primula vulgaris*).

Many-zoned Polypore (*Coriolus versicolor*).

In making the drawings for the colour plates, too, I tried to find typical examples, because I soon realised when I started really *looking* at trees, that within certain specific limits they manifested a remarkable degree of variety and individuality. Extreme examples of this are the 'sports', such as the German Copper Beech from which all present-day Copper Beeches descend, but I found one Common Oak whose leaves always remained pale green right through the summer, another whose lammas shoots were invariably coloured crimson, and yet another whose acorns hung down on stalks twice the normal length. I also came across a grove of Crack Willows whose leaves were so much larger than the average that it was some time before I could convince myself of their identity. The Elms too, provided a wealth of eccentricities, including one form of *U. carpinifolia* which lacked the usual pendulous branchlets and whose abundant fruits were bright yellow, suffused with crimson in the area of the seed cavity, which gave the trees a very distinctive tawny appearance in the spring. All the latter, alas, were killed by Dutch Elm disease during the 1970s, though perhaps a clone from one of them may still linger, undetected, in some hedgerow, ready to spring up again should the disease recede and the all-devouring hedge-cutter spare it.

Occasionally, I have used material from very vigorous young growth or sucker shoots where, as in the case of the sharply lobed sucker leaves of White Poplar or the Holly-like leaves of the Holm Oak, these are frequently encountered yet vary considerably from the typical leaves in the crown of the tree; or, as in the case of the Turkey Oak, where the characteristics scarcely apparent in the very small buds from a mature tree are conveniently magnified by use of a vigorous young shoot.

Many people who are not particularly interested in trees tend to identify them chiefly by their leaves, or in winter by their twigs and buds, and would find it hard, in many cases, to describe their flowers. The exceptions are such trees as the Wild Cherry, Hawthorn and Horse Chestnut, with their showy blossoms; the Limes, whose aromatic flowers, beloved of bees, appear in midsummer when people get out and about, taking more notice of nature; and Pussy Willow and Hazel, whose catkins provide a welcome and familiar foretaste of spring. I hope, therefore, that the illustrations in this book will encourage people to seek out some of the more neglected tree flowers, many of which are very beautiful although they may occur early in the year, like the glowing crimson male catkins of the Black and hybrid Black Poplars, or the hairy purple and brown catkins of the Aspen. The small but numerous flowers of the Elms impart a distinctive reddish-purple haze over much of the lowland landscape in late February and March, and the tassels of lime-green Oak catkins add their special flavour to the woodlands and hedgerows in May.

The colour plates were all done from freshly gathered specimens, using an H pencil in the first instance, on white card or hot-pressed paper, then putting on a wash of the palest colour present, and slowly building up the colour, using a minimum amount of water, in anything up to half a dozen layers where a high degree of opacity was needed. I used no body colour except in a very few instances, preferring to rely on the white paper or pale primary wash to provide the highlights, but white

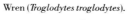
Wren (*Troglodytes troglodytes*).

petals were painted first with Chinese white to help differentiate them from their background, and then shaded with a variety of colour mixtures: it is surprising how much the shadows on white petals of different flowers can vary in tone. The most difficult specimens to draw and paint, as anyone who has painted roses will appreciate, were those delicate blossoms whose rapid growth, once they had recovered from the temporary wilting caused by being plucked and removed to an alien environment, resulted in fugitive shapes and colours that could only be countered by working very fast. Of these awkward models, the worst, so far as colour changes went, was the Horse Chestnut, the corollas of whose very numerous and complex flowers progressed, almost before my eyes, from yellow through orange to crimson pink, while the flowers of the Wild Cherry, basking in the April sunlight that streamed through my study window, opened their petals so fast that I could hardly keep up with them even in the drawing, and had to use fresh models for some of the flowers when I came to paint them.

A word on the vexed question of taxonomy: in recent years most natural orders have undergone a continuous process of alteration at generic and particularly at specific levels as fresh knowledge or improved systems of classification have led to new groupings. In the Synopsis I have, I hope, given the most up-to-date name of each species, variety or hybrid. Authors' names are included and, in some cases, the name is followed by its synonym where this is very familiar from long use in older works of reference. The English names are, in most instances, well established, but where there are several commonly employed I have used the best-known in the text and given the alternatives in the Synopsis.

Finally, I have tried to avoid the excessive use of technical terms in the captions to the plates, but I have had to make use of a few where there is no alternative word, as in the parts of the flower, or where not to adopt them would result in a clumsy or imprecise description. In such cases, reference can be made to the Glossary.

Wherever land is left to its own devices, apart from the most inhospitable sites, such as stagnant bogs or high mountains, it will quickly be colonised by trees. Seeds are borne on the wind, carried by birds and land animals, or washed up on the banks of streams and rivers. To ensure this continuity, a tree, in the course of a long lifetime, will produce vast quantities of seeds, only a tiny proportion of which will germinate, let alone survive to maturity. Of all the agents which militate against the chances of a seedling's survival, man is the most active and indefatigable. Today, he has at his command machinery that makes the process of forest clearance easier and faster than ever before; and as the human population continues to expand, so the demand for land on which to grow food crops becomes even more urgent. In this country, it was a bitter twist of fate that the arrival of a new and deadly strain of Dutch Elm disease should coincide with a period when trees and hedgerows were already disappearing at an unprecedented rate. Never before has there been so pressing a need to conserve what forest areas still remain to us — bearing in mind that the term 'forest', as understood by foresters, comprises any area of woodland from huge tracts down to the smallest copse or spinney. Trees provide shelter, food and breeding habitat for a huge number of species of both fauna and flora. To ensure their preservation should be the vital concern of every person who has ever enjoyed the sound of a bird singing, the sight of a butterfly on the wing, a wild flower growing, or indeed anything else in nature.

Juvenile Little Owl (*Athene noctua*).

THE TREES

THE BEECH

The Beech, being both useful as a timber tree and exceedingly handsome, has been widely planted. Yet although specimens are to be found almost anywhere in the British Isles, it is native only on the chalk and limestone soils of south and south-eastern England, and it is in these regions that it achieves its greatest glory.

As a boy, I spent much of my holiday time at a cousin's house in Wiltshire. The house nestled among low hills between the northern edge of Salisbury Plain and the Vale of Avon. The vale itself was Elm country — a patchwork of small fields divided by thick hedges where these trees grew abundantly; but on the plain and in the woods that clothed its steep escarpment, the Beech reigned supreme. Behind my cousin's house the ground rose sharply in a series of artificial terraces which were miniature replicas of the prehistoric lynchets cut into the face of the downs to the south. At the top of the terraces was a wood of some five or six acres which consisted chiefly of tall Beech trees, though there were Oaks and Elms and Ashes around its fringes, and at its northern end a long dark avenue of Yews and Hornbeams. The Beeches were mature trees with massive, clean boles that rose up like the columns of a Romanesque cathedral, smooth, grey and round, inviting to the touch. High above, their branches spread out to form a natural vaulting, and here, in their swaying tops, a colony of Rooks nested. In early spring, while the Rooks fed their young amid a constant babble of caws and cackles, the lower part of the wood became carpeted with Primroses. Later came the Bluebells, while the long, pointed, shiny-brown buds of the Beeches would break open and the pale green leaves, so soft, silken and immaculate, would emerge and unfurl. In May, when the sun shone, a myriad shafts of light struck down through the canopy, and the tiers of translucent leaves shone as though carved from the finest laminae of peridot and beryl.

As summer progressed, the leaves hardened and became opaque; the wood was then a cool and shady place, where little sunlight filtered through, and few plants could thrive on the forest floor. Only at the edges of the wood, where the sun could gain entry, were there dense beds of Nettles and tall Bracken, and bushes of nut, thorn and Holly.

In the autumn, however, the wood once more became a place of colour: at first green and chrome yellow, later with an increasing admixture of orange-brown and coppery tones. And as the leaves came pattering down to lie in deep drifts in the rides, the mast – glossy dark brown nuts in their hard, bristly capsules – also fell; and all manner of birds and small mammals, mindful of the lean winter days ahead, came to share in the feast and carry off booty to be stored against hard times.

I have a picture in my mind of the wood in deep midwinter, when the trees stand dark and gaunt, and their feathery twigs make a filigree pattern against a colourless, marmoreal sky, while the Rooks' nests sway perilously back and forth. The wind moans softly in their tops, and in the west the brazen disc of the sun sinks towards the horizon. Then the Rooks, who have been out foraging by day, come soaring high above the wood in a great noisy, untidy, joyous throng and drop, like so many falling leaves, swooping and floating and side-slipping towards their roost; and there is a loud gabble of sound as they jostle and squabble over their favourite perches before they tuck their heads under their wings, and settle down for the night.

THE OAKS

For some ten years I lived in a house in a north Essex village. From its windows I could see a great many Oaks, some of them in parkland, others in woodland or bordering the lane beside the house. Whatever their age, they were always easily recognisable, even in winter; yet they showed strong individuality, and the older they became, the more marked were their idiosyncrasies. As I got to know them I found that they differed not just in the disposition of their trunks and branches (such differences sometimes being attributable to pruning, pollarding or browsing by cattle), but in many small particulars governed only by genetic make-up, several examples of which I have given in the Introduction.

On the other side of the lane from my house there was a wood of about

BEECH
I
FAGUS SYLVATICA

Fig.1

Beech twigs are dark purplish-brown and the long, sharply pointed chestnut-brown buds, many-scaled and alternately set, make the tree easily identifiable in winter

Fig.2

The buds swell and elongate considerably before leaf-burst towards the end of April.

Fig.3

Twig on 30th April, with young leaves and male catkins emerging together.

Fig.4

Young leaves from a rather meagre twig on 3rd May. They are pale green and fringed with long, silky hairs which soon disappear.

Beech (*Fagus sylvatica*).

Fig. 2

Fig. 4

Fig. 3

Fig. 1

II

Fig. 1

Twig with male and female catkins on 11th May. The male catkins, which are soon shed, hang down like tassels, and consist of dense bunches of stamens with greenish anthers, each separate flower enclosed by purplish bracts.

Fig. 2

Leaves and fruit on 13th July. The leaves are now dark, glossy green above, paler beneath, having wavy margins and parallel veins. The base of each leaf is slightly unequal. Fruits are hard capsules covered with long, reflexed bristles.

Fig. 3

Leaf of 'Copper Beech'.

Fig. 4

Ripe fruit in October. The capsule has split open to release (generally) two hard, chestnut-brown seeds which are triangular in section.

Fig. 5

Beech is capable of magnificent autumn colour, with green, yellow and copper-brown in early November. Before falling, they will have turned a deep, rich orange-brown.

Fig. 1

Fig. 2

Fig. 3

Fig. 4

Fig. 5

twenty-five acres. It consisted mainly of European Larch, but parts of it were made up of mixed broad-leaves, and all around its perimeter were ancient Oaks as well as other large trees and much Bramble and Hazel coppice, suggesting that woodland had occupied the site long before the Larches were planted. Immediately opposite the house there was a very handsome Oak tree, perhaps two hundred years old and still healthy and full of vigour. I marked its progress through the seasons, year after year, and whenever I looked up into its branches or at the bank from which it sprang, I would invariably notice some creature or plant which relied on it wholly or principally for food, shelter or other form of sustenance. That's the great thing about the Oak: it is the most hospitable, most generous of all our trees, somehow managing to maintain its own strength and vigour while supporting a multitude of other life-forms.

In that part of East Anglia, Oak, Ash, Elm and Sycamore were the four principal species of the landscape, both in hedgerows and in woodlands, but there was a great variety of other trees as well. In this respect we were more fortunate than some parts of the country, where Elm was by far the predominant species, when the virulent form of Dutch Elm disease struck in the early 1970s. The Elms died, alas, and are still dying, but sufficient trees remained (where they had not already been removed by farmers) to maintain an impoverished, but still a reasonably well-wooded landscape.

The Oaks were nearly all Common or Pedunculate Oaks *(Quercus robur)*. The Sessile Oak *(Q. petraea)*, which largely replaces *Q. robur* in parts of the country, notably areas of Wales and the north-west, is a very similar tree, also a native, and performs much the same ecological function. But it is uncommon in East Anglia and I was lucky to find one local specimen, from which I gathered the specimens of leaf, flower and fruit to draw. It grew at the edge of a nearby wood, surrounded by Ash and Common Oak, and I often wondered what odd chance had brought this comparative stranger, either as acorn, seedling or transplant, to this spot.

In addition to our two native species of Oak, three introduced species are sometimes encountered. Of these, the least likely to be found outside parks and gardens is the American Red Oak (not illustrated), although I have occasionally come across specimens in mixed woodland, and more

Pedunculate Oak (*Quercus robur*).

frequently as a colourful screen around the edges of large forest plantations, hiding the drabness of the conifers beyond.

The evergreen Holm Oak *(Q. ilex)* is much commoner, and has even become naturalised in a few favoured situations around the south coast of England. In a wood near my house there are several good specimens growing together with Holly, and the superficial similarity of the two species is soon evident. ('Holm' derives from the Anglo-Saxon word for Holly, and *ilex* is the Latin word for the same plant.) Even on close inspection, they can easily be confused, for leaves in the lower part of the tree often have spiny edges, remarkably like those of Holly.

The Turkey Oak *(Q. cerris),* commonest of the three, is thoroughly naturalised in many parts of the British Isles, and in my own neighbourhood I have found it in woodland, in hedgerows, as a park tree and self-sown on the banks of old railway lines. It is a tall and very handsome tree, but not being a native, it falls far short of our own Oaks as a host to other species. Unfortunately, one creature that it does harbour is a Gall Wasp; although the insect leaves the Turkey Oak unscathed, its second generation causes disfiguring Knopper Galls on the acorns of our native Oaks.

Oaks are to be found almost everywhere in Britain, except in the most inhospitable highlands and northern isles; and since they are trees of such

PEDUNCULATE OAK

I

QUERCUS ROBUR

Fig. 1

A straight Oak twig taken in midwinter from vigorous young coppice growth and showing clearly the many-scaled, bluntly pointed brown buds arranged in a spiral, with the characteristic cluster of buds at the apex of the twig.

Fig. 2

Gnarled twig from a mature tree on 16th April. The buds are just starting to swell, the bud scales uncovering paler areas as they expand.

Fig. 3

Ten days later, the buds have more than doubled in size. The spiral pattern of the imbricated bud scales is now plain to see.

Fig. 4

Towards the end of April, the buds burst and tufts of delicate pale green leaves emerge and start to unfold.

Fig. 5

From other buds, leaves and male catkins appear simultaneously.

Thrush's Anvil, (shells of *Cepaea nemoralis*)
and Oak leaves with
Spangle and Silk-button Galls.

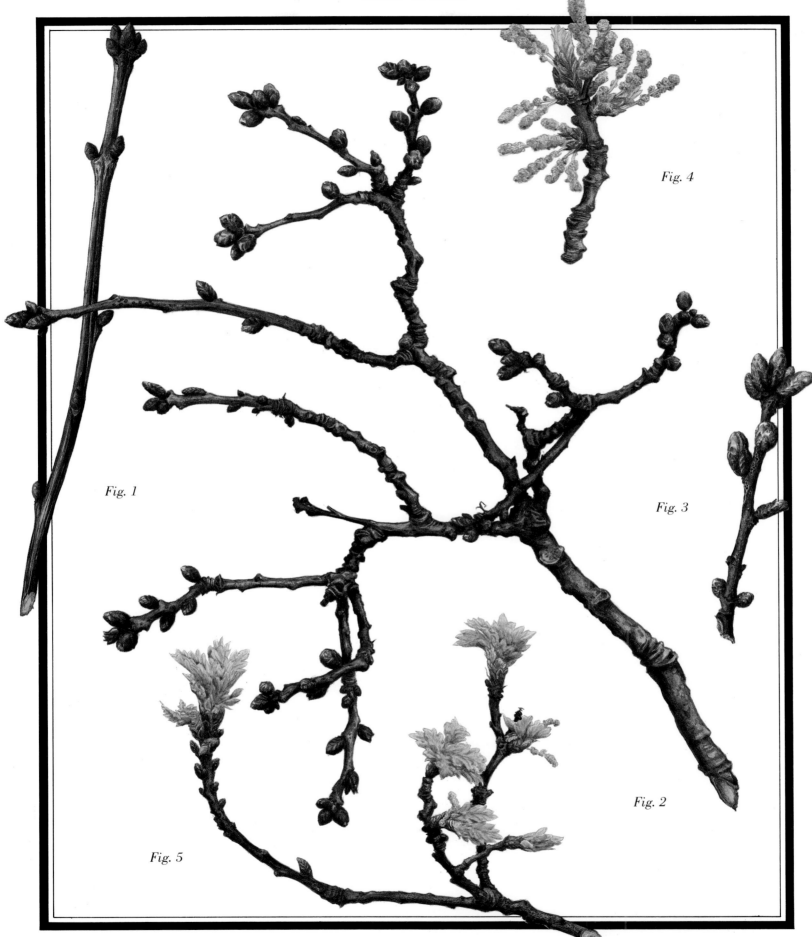

Fig. 4

Fig. 1

Fig. 3

Fig. 2

Fig. 5

II

Fig. 1

Shoot on 13th May, the soft young leaves growing fast and frequently, at this stage, tinged with pale brownish crimson. Hanging down from the shoot are the long yellow-green catkins which bear the male flowers in the form of tiny clusters of stamens and even smaller bracts. Near the tip of the twigs, borne on long stalks (the peduncles which give this species its name) can be seen the very inconspicuous female flowers, the globular ovaries enclosed by bracts from which dark crimson stigmas protrude.

Fig. 2

Leaves, now dark green and leathery in texture, and the fully developed fruits, in early September. The fruit is the familiar green acorn in its shallow cup, two or three of which alternate on a stalk several inches long. The lobed leaves are borne on very short stalks, and have a smooth surface; whereas the leaf of the Sessile Oak is tapered at its base, that of the Pedunculate Oak is distinguished by a pair of ear-like lobes, or auricles.

Fig. 3

By the end of September, leaves here and there may be fading and beginning to turn brown. Their under-surfaces will almost certainly be covered with the tiny discs of Spangle or Silk-button Galls. By now the acorns have also turned brown, and are starting to drop. Sometimes the cups will fall too, but many remain on the tree through the winter.

Fig. 4

The bright, copper-brown autumn leaf in early November. These may be retained on the tree well into the winter.

Marble Gall (*Adleria kollari*).

Fig. 2

Fig. 1

Fig. 4

Fig. 3

SESSILE OAK

QUERCUS PETRAEA

Fig. 1

Twig of Sessile Oak with leaves and flowers on 1st June. The male catkins, which are similar to those of *Q. robur,* have shed their pollen and turned brown, but female flowers can be seen in leaf axils towards the apex of the twig. Similar in form to those of *Q. robur,* they are sessile or sub-sessile, while those of *Q. robur* are carried on long stalks. Conversely, the leaves of Sessile Oak are stalked, while those of Pedunculate Oak are sessile. They also differ in being tapered or rounded at the base and lacking the prominent auricles of *Q. robur.* (Axillary buds on this specimen are abnormal, being deformed by galls.)

Fig. 2

Leaves and fruit on 28th August. The acorns of Sessile Oak are either sessile or carried on very short stalks, and they are shorter than those of Pedunculate Oak.

Sessile Oak (*Quercus petraea*).

Fig. 1

Fig. 2

TURKEY OAK
I

QUERCUS CERRIS

Fig. 1

Winter twig from a mature tree. The twigs are a dark, dull brown, in colour, the buds very small, pale brown and surrounded by long, twisted stipules. As with other Oaks, there is a cluster of buds at the apex of each shoot.

Fig. 2

Winter twig from a vigorous young tree, showing all the typical features, but in an exaggerated form.

Fig. 3

Twig with buds swelling in late April.

Fig. 4

Young leaves and male catkins emerging together on 10th May.

Turkey Oak (*Quercus cerris*).

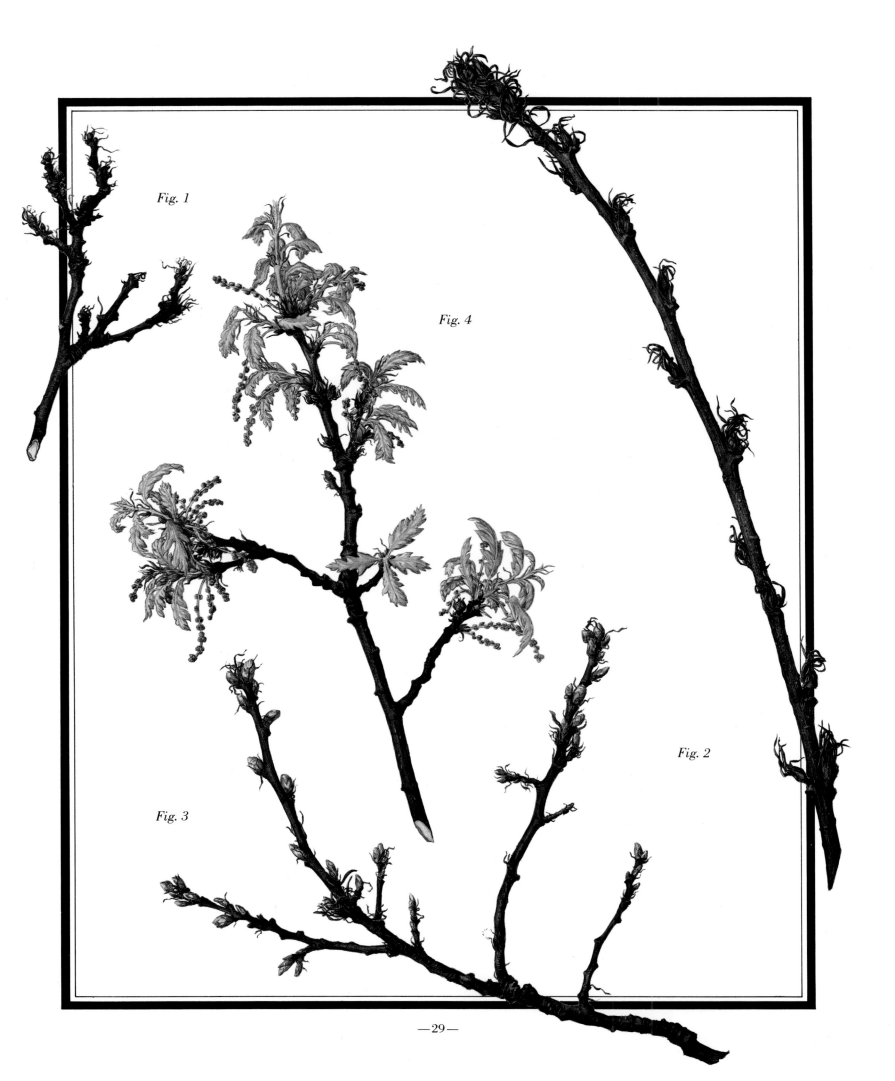

Fig. 1

Fig. 4

Fig. 2

Fig. 3

Fig.1

Twig with young leaves and fully extended male catkins on 15th May. The leaves at this stage, faintly tinged with pink or brown above and covered with a grey-green pubescence underneath, give the tree a characteristic colour when seen from a distance. Acorns of Turkey Oak take two years to develop; two produced last year, and due to ripen this year, can be seen at the second node from the base of the twig.

Fig.2

On 24th May, a section of new growth with leaves cut away to show the very inconspicuous greenish-yellow female flowers, almost hidden by long stipules, which arise from the leaf axils, and which will develop into acorns in the following year.

Fig.3

Leaves and acorns on 19th September. The leaves are dark green and glossy, longer, narrower and more evenly lobed than the leaves of *Q. robur*. The acorns are instantly recognisable by their mossy cups.

Fig.4

Fallen acorn in October, mahogany-brown with a pale disc at its base.

Fig.5

Leaves of typical rich yellow to orange-brown colour on 23rd October,

Fig.6

Occasional leaves, especially on young growth, may be deeply cut between the lobes.

Fig. 2

Fig. 1

Fig. 4

Fig. 3

Fig. 6

Fig. 5

HOLM OAK

QUERCUS ILEX

The Holm Oak is evergreen and here we see the dark-coloured old leaves, one dead leaf ready to fall, and a shoot with young, newly emerged leaves, as well as numerous male catkins, on 11th June.

At about the same date, a twig showing female flowers on straight stalks growing from the axils of two of the leaves. These flowers will take two years to develop into acorns. Fawn stipules growing from leaf axils surround minute buds.

Fig. 3

Fruiting on 5th October. The leaves are lanceolate with wavy edges and a few teeth, dark green above and thickly felted white on the undersides. By winter most of this pubescence will have worn off and undersides of leaves will be grey-green. Nearly two-thirds of each pointed acorn is enclosed by its cup. Below, left, is a ripe acorn on 18th October.

Fig. 4

Leaves from young trees, low branches of old trees and epicormic shoots are often sharply spined, resembling Holly leaves.

Fig. 1

Fig. 2

Fig. 3

Fig. 4

strong character, individual trees are often remembered well, associated perhaps with certain experiences or with special places. One such recollection, in this instance of an Oak wood rather than of a single tree, is especially vivid.

Many years ago, on my first spring fishing holiday in Devonshire, I stayed at a quiet little inn which stood among hanging woodlands on the slopes leading down from Exmoor, only two or three miles by a narrow, winding road from the sea. From my bedroom, at night, I could hear the babble of the little river across the road, and I woke to the sounds of a Song Thrush singing from a blossomed bough close by and the calls of Cuckoos echoing across the valley. It was a place where you breathed sweet, clean air all day, came home ravenous for dinner and slept soundly all night.

One day I had been fishing up on the moor where the streams purled over wide boulder-strewn beds and shafts of sunlight struck fiery sparks from the amber depths of the pools. It had been fine, but no fish were rising and I decided to try the lower part of the river, near the inn. I clambered down the steepest part of the escarpment which consisted of a forest of gnarled Oaks, all of them shagged with grey and orange lichens, where the river plunged through rocky ravines in a series of miniature cataracts, and the pools were deep and cold and inky green. The banks and the rocky walls of the stream were rich in lush growths of ferns of many species, and an abundance of mosses and liverworts. Soon I was absorbed in botanising.

Busy collecting specimens for later identification, I had not been aware of the weather. Now I looked up and saw that the sky above me was livid, the twisted branches of the Oaks, hoary with ash-grey lichen, standing out whitely against it. At the same moment I heard the first distant peal of thunder.

I looked around for some shelter, and had just decided that an overhanging rock beside the stream would offer better protection than the trees, when the storm broke. The ragged edge of a great purplish-blue cloud mass spread rapidly across the sky, and darkness, like a premature dusk, covered the scene. It became very still; leaves hung limp and the bird song died away. There was only the muted roar of the river and the thunder rumbling on querulously from different points on the horizon. Looking around me, I had the feeling that all the living forms of the forest —

trees, ferns, birds, insects – were holding their breath; it was rather like being in a church, awaiting the first crashing chords of some jubilant anthem. When, in fact, the silence was broken, the effect was no less dramatic. A chill breath of wind, which set the young Oak leaves a-flutter and sent a shiver down my spine, was followed by a flash of lightning, briefly etching the trees in sharp relief, and then a clap of thunder like a mighty hammer blow on some giant's anvil; and as its reverberations slowly died away, the first big drops of rain came splashing down, hitting the branches of the trees and breaking into quicksilver fragments. I made for my shelter beside a pool fed by a small waterfall. The flat ledge on which I stood was overhung by rock and twisted tree roots from which plume-like fronds of Lady Fern reached outwards in graceful tufts. The first big rain drops made rings on the pool's surface which spread and overlapped in an elegant pattern of concentric circles, but as they multiplied the patterns became fused, and soon the whole pool was whipped into a froth of broken water. The rain came teeming down so thickly that it made a mist, blotting out the more distant trees, and with such violence that every leaf, branch and grass blade trembled and shuddered under its impact.

Crouching under my rocky shelter, I peered out through a dripping screen, awed by the ferocity of the storm yet fascinated by the spectacle – the almost solid wall of water exploding into a crystalline vapour as it hit the trees and the ground. The river roared louder than ever as its volume increased, and the clear, deep pools were stained with brown and turbid water from the peaty moors above. Debris started to come down: sticks and small branches and skeletal tufts of heather, and the waterfalls swelled into a foamy lather which spread out across the pools, broke up and sailed away and out of sight like giant soapsuds.

After some ten minutes, the lashing, drenching fury of the storm started to abate. Very gradually, the amorphous body of descending water separated once more into silvery streaks of individual raindrops. Suddenly, the sun broke out from behind the receding pall of cloud, and all was sparkle and glitter, every leaf and twig embellished with brilliant droplets of water that shone with all the colours of the prism. Everything dripped and oozed, tiny rivulets meandered across the forest floor, clouds of vapour rose from the ground and the rocks as they were warmed anew by the sun's rays, and with the steam there came a delicious scent of earth, moss and rich vegetable decay. Life returned to the treetops as the birds tentatively resumed their songs, and while the last of the rain pattered innocuously among the Oak leaves, a rainbow arched across the valley.

THE SWEET CHESTNUT

Although the Sweet Chestnut produces very strong and durable timber, it is seldom used in large sizes as the wood tends to exhibit spiral graining and 'shakes' or faults, causing wastage in sawing. However, the chapel of an ancient priory within a few miles of my house has massive roof beams of Sweet Chestnut, which — for reasons I have never discovered — harbour no spiders.

More usually, the species is grown as a coppiced crop cut on a rotation of twelve to fifteen years for the production of hop-poles, fencing stakes, gate-posts, palings and the like; and the Chestnut copse with which I am most familiar was used for this purpose — to produce fencing stakes for the farm — up to about fifteen years ago. The coppice stools from which the stakes were cut were interspersed with mature trees, and this system, known as 'coppice with standards' was once widely employed — for other useful species such as Oak and Ash as well as Chestnut; the result was a kind of woodland, now all too rare, which provided a good habitat for wildlife and the very best conditions for an interesting and varied flora. It always gave me pleasure to watch the straight, clean boles of the coppice stools being cut when their time came, then taken down to the yard to be trimmed up and pointed ready for use after they had dried out for six months or so in the stack. Of course, the system is still used, since there is a continuing demand for Chestnut stakes, but for the most part only in very large-scale enterprises. Not many farms today are self-sufficient in timber products, labour forces being too small, and the few remaining farm workers tending to be adept with a spanner but little skilled in the use of woodland tools.

That small wood of Chestnut coppice — it was known as the Chestnut Grove — stood above a narrow, deep lane, on the other side of which was a larger area of very ill-drained mixed woodland choked with the debris of fallen trees, with Bracken on the drier slopes and jungles of man-high Horsetail in the hollows. Above the Chestnuts was some hilly pastureland, bounded by two other woods, one of which, known as the Round Grove, had a large Badger set along its northern edge. I remember spending some chilly hours on a moonlit night in early summer, crouched beside the bole of one of the big trees in the Chestnut Grove, waiting to see the Badgers emerge. The night was full of small noises: Owls hooting in the distance, rustlings of tiny rodents among the dead leaves, some Peewits — the most wakeful of birds — calling plaintively as they flew overhead, the bleating of lambs from down the lane, the low, answering calls of the ewes, and the loud, crunching noise of a herd of beef cows and their calves as they grazed their way across the grassland in front of me.

I missed the moment when the first Badger emerged from the mouth of its set. All of a sudden it was there, just its head and shoulders showing, its muzzle lifted and questing from side to side to catch any hint of an alien presence borne on the breeze. Long seconds passed before it heaved itself out onto the grass; then it turned back to sniff at the opening, and presently it was followed by three cubs. I watched them avidly through binoculars for fifteen minutes or so as they rooted along the edge of the wood, their forms appearing and vanishing among the moon-shadows of the trees, but gradually they disappeared into the darkness beneath the tall Beeches, and were gone.

Fallen leaves and fruit husks of Sweet Chestnut.

SWEET CHESTNUT
I

CASTANEA SATIVA

Fig.1

Sweet Chestnut twig in winter. It is stout, angular, with prominent ridges, and the rather squat greenish-brown buds are arranged spirally.

Fig.2

Slender twig from a low branch of a tree grown in close woodland. A casual glance suggests that the buds are arranged alternately rather than in a spiral, which can be confusing to anyone trying to identify the tree.

Fig.3

Twig with swelling buds in mid-April. The pinkish-brown colour of this twig is very typical of the species.

Fig.4

Young leaves starting to emerge on 20th April.

Sweet Chestnut (*Castanea sativa*).

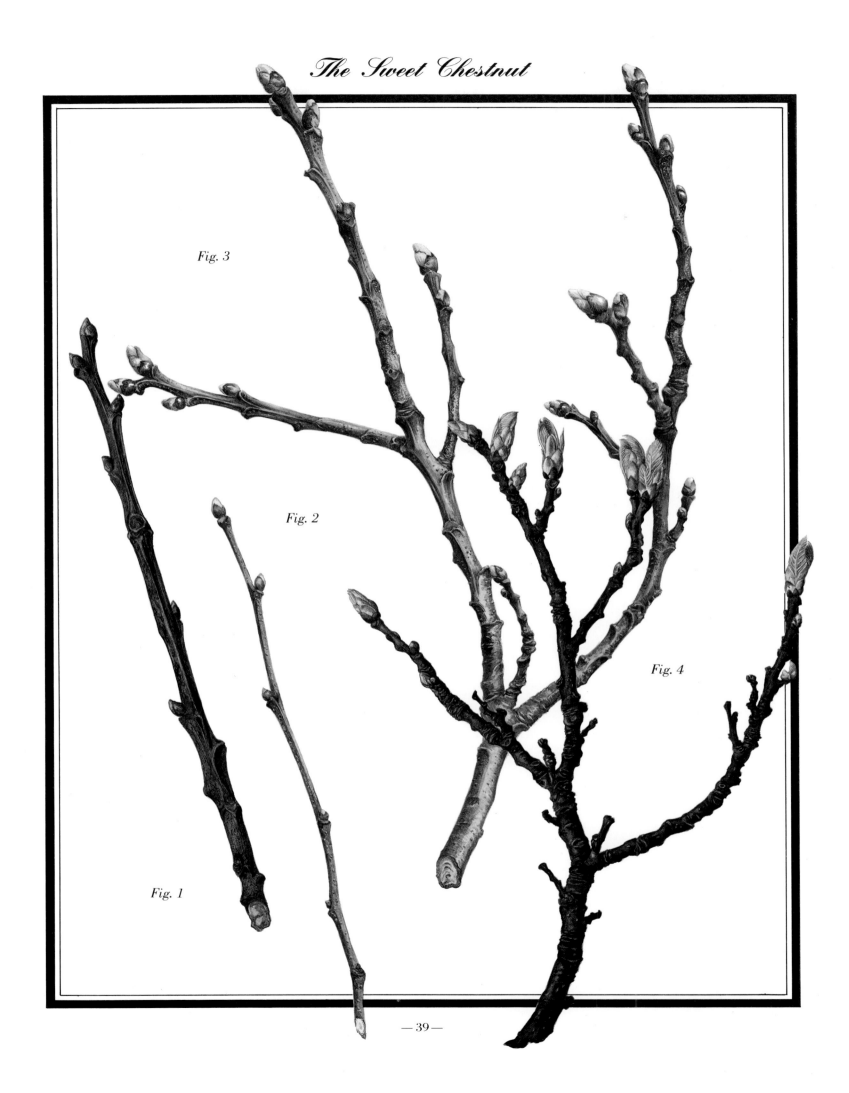

Fig. 3

Fig. 2

Fig. 4

Fig. 1

Fig.1

The male and female flowers of Sweet Chestnut (seen here early in July) are unusual in being borne on the same catkins. The small male flowers, with their yellow anthers, are carried in little bunches along most of the catkin's length; the female flowers, if present, are identifiable by their larger size and tufts of long cream-coloured styles, and are borne near the base of the catkin.

Fig.2

Leaves and fruit in September. The leaves are shiny green with prominent veining and large teeth, and may be 10″ long or more. Occasionally they are lobed at the base. The fruits consist of rounded husks, thickly covered with sharp yellowish-green spines. Dried-up male catkins are still attached to them.

Fig.3

Ripe fruit in late October, with the capsule split open to reveal three nuts, the one on the left very plump, the centre one abortive and that on the right with one concave surface. The nut is glossy brown with a tuft of shrivelled styles at its apex.

Fig.4

Typical autumn colour is a rich yellow which gradually turns to brown.

Fig. 1.

Fig. 3.

Fig. 2.

Fig. 4.

THE BIRCHES

Few people are aware that there is more than one species of Birch growing wild in these islands, nor does it really matter, for although Hairy Birch tends to grow on damper sites, both trees, on the whole, favour a similar terrain and are physically very alike. The most important of several distinguishing features, for all but very young trees, is that Silver Birch has a pendulous habit while Hairy Birch does not.

There are many parts of southern England where Birches do grow naturally and profusely, but I tend to associate them, on the whole, with suburban gardens, where their hanging shoots caress the heads of garden gnomes, or with the heathy countryside around Camberley, where I spent my early schooldays and for which I have no great affection. I prefer to think of them in Scotland, where they conjure up all sorts of pleasant memories, mainly of fishing holidays, but also of botanising expeditions, particularly in search of fungi, for the Birch is, with the possible exception of the Beech, host to more species of fungi than any other tree.

One such occasion, on some moorland not far from Loch Lomond where there were Birch trees (and also Beeches planted along the boundary fences), proved especially exciting because not only did I find a great many fungi, including Scarlet Flycap, Panther Cap, Chanterelle and many types of Boletus and Milk Cap, but I also spent an anxious ten minutes watching, and making sketches of, a small bird which *seemed* to be the very rare Little Bunting. Unfortunately, I am not a sufficiently expert ornithologist ever to have been quite certain of the identification, and it must remain one of those frustrating mysteries which all amateur naturalists encounter from time to time.

More recently, I was fishing the Spey above Grantown in the last weeks of the season, and on a day when the river was in spate and unfishable, taking a leisurely walk along its banks, I came to a long, narrow stretch of meadowland with many fine mature Silver Birches. There were Birches too, on the banks of the river, but mixed with Wych Elms, Rowans and Bird Cherries whose leaves had already turned to orange and crimson. Dotted among the tussocks of meadow grass were innumerable white Puff-balls and patches of Field Mushrooms, and I gathered a hat-full of both for next

Silver Birch (*Betula pendula*).

day's breakfast. The river came down in an angry, swirling flood, and I sat on the trunk of a fallen tree to make a sketch, trying in vain to catch that sensation of inexorable power conveyed by its smooth, steely-grey surface, broken here and there by eddies and cat's-paws, bobbing pieces of timber and flotillas of bubbles, all travelling along at a furious rate.

THE ALDER

The Alder, though common enough in the vicinity of water, is not very familiar to the public at large. The tree is densely twigged and, until quite old, conical in shape. Its bark, its leaves, and its fruits that are hard and cone-like, are all very dark in colour. In winter these characteristics often cause the Alder to be mistaken for a conifer.

I visualise Alders in three different types of habitat, and in each of these they take on an entirely different appearance and character.

The first is an Essex wood, or carr, which I used to know very well. I love woods, perhaps more than any other kind of environment. They are places where you can be alone, they are nearly always beautiful (young plantations of pure conifer may be an exception), and they provide plenty of interest for the naturalist. The added attraction is that owing to differences, however slight, in soil, aspect, climate, elevation, drainage and other factors, no two woods are ever identical.

This particular wood, some seven acres in extent, was very wet when I first knew it, the drainage ditches being full of silt and clogged with tree

SILVER BIRCH

BETULA PENDULA

Fig. 1

The twigs of Silver Birch are long, thin and whippy; they are without hairs but covered with little warts, and vary in colour from reddish-brown to grey. The buds are small, narrow, pointed and tend to be slightly curved; they may be brown or green. Besides buds, the winter twigs display the short, brown, immature male catkins which have developed during the previous summer.

Fig. 2

Twig in the first week of May. Leaves and catkins have emerged simultaneously. The small, erect, green catkins bear the female flowers; the longer, pendulous catkins at the tip of the twig are male, and have reached the stage where they are starting to shed their pollen.

Fig. 3

Twig drawn on 9th July. The small leaves are triangular or diamond-shaped and have doubly toothed edges. The ripening female catkins are still green but have now become fat and pendulous. The small green catkins at the tips of the new shoots are next year's male catkins.

Fig. 4

Twig on 25th October. By this time, most of the leaves have turned a fine rich yellow. Others are still yellowing from the edges inwards. The immature male catkins have changed from green to brown, while most of the ripe fruit catkins — also brown by now — will have fallen from the tree (though in sheltered situations they may remain on the tree much longer). A ripe catkin, in the process of breaking up to dispense its seed, is shown above the autumn twig, together with a fruit bract, shaped like a fleur-de-lis, and a group of the tiny, winged seeds.

Fig. 1

Fig. 2

Fig. 3

Fig. 4

HAIRY BIRCH

BETULA PUBESCENS

Fig. 1

The twigs of Hairy Birch are brown or greenish-grey, duller than those of Silver Birch, and instead of the warts which cover the latter, they are clothed, particularly toward their tips, with short greyish hairs. Buds and immature male catkins are similar to those of Silver Birch.

Fig. 2

Twig on 24th April, with growth buds starting to break open and male catkins swelling and extending.

Fig. 3

By 1st May, young leaves and erect, green, female catkins have emerged. The male catkins are growing fast, but are not yet fully extended. When in full flower, they are similar to those of Silver Birch.

Fig. 4

Twig of Hairy Birch on 26th July, with ripening female catkins and, at its tip, one immature male catkin. The leaves tend to be somewhat larger than those of Silver Birch and more rounded, and the edges are more evenly toothed.

Fig. 5

Autumn leaves and ripe fruits on 15th September.

Hairy Birch (*Betula pubescens*).

Fig. 2

Fig. 3

Fig. 4

Fig. 1

Fig. 5

ALDER
I

ALNUS GLUTINOSA

Fig.1

Alder twig on 24th November, just after the last leaves have been shed, showing growth buds, male and (much smaller) female immature catkins, and the woody, cone-like fruits, a group of seeds from which appears below. These seeds are generally carried by water to some suitable muddy bank where they can germinate.

Fig.2

Winter twig, showing more clearly the spirally arranged, two-scaled, often purplish buds, each of which is borne on a short stalk.

Fig.3

Male and female catkins on 10th March. The female flowers are small, crimson, and made up of tiny, overlapping bracts and protruding stigmas. The long male catkins are very handsome, yellow and deep crimson.

Fig.4

Bud burst on 19th April.

Fig. 1

Fig. 2

Fig. 3

Fig. 4

II

Fig.1

Leafy twig of Alder on 14th September, bearing immature male and female catkins which will mature the following spring. The leaves are rounded with a tapering base and a notch at the apex.

Fig.2

Another twig, about the same date, bearing female catkins of the current year, which are by now hard, and starting to turn brown. These will open to release their seeds during the autumn. The Alder does not display any autumn colour, the leaves simply fading and then turning dark brown after they have fallen.

Alder (*Alnus glutinosa*).

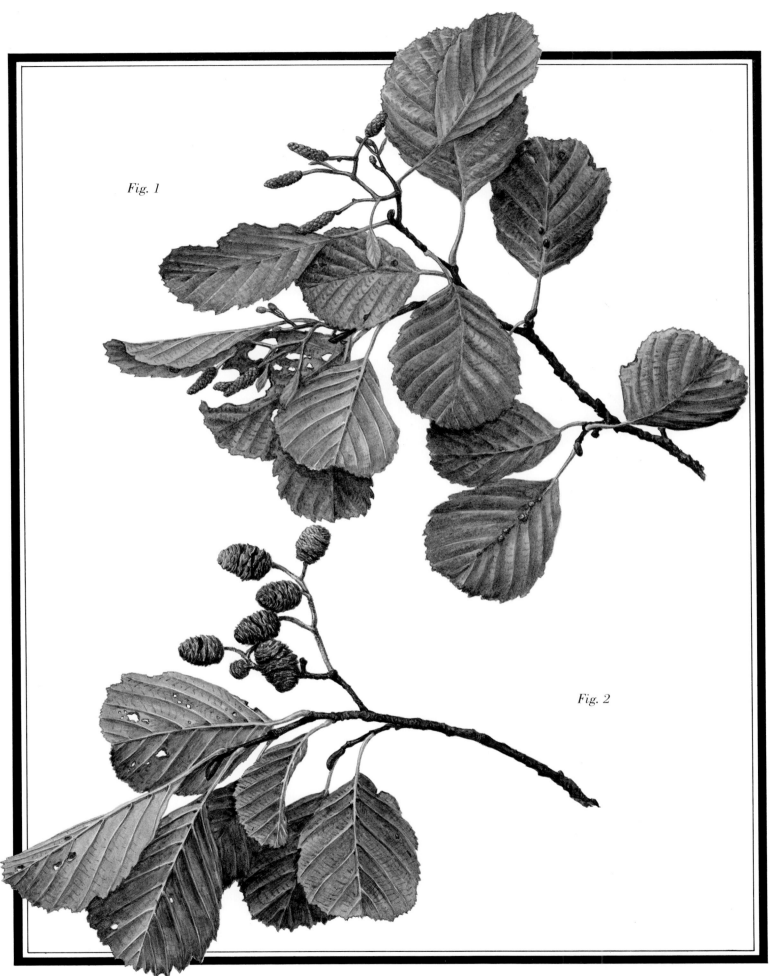

Fig. 1

Fig. 2

roots and other debris, and the lower part almost a bog. At its upper end was a dry bank, through which ran the main path, bordered by Smooth-leaved and Wych Elms. On this higher ground there were some good Ashes, which gradually petered out, to be replaced by Alders, with occasional White Willows and Sallow bushes. The Alders were very straight and tall, with thin crowns, and some were clothed with Ivy. Beneath their high, dark canopy the wood, in summer, was a dreamy place of lush vegetation and steamy, stagnant pools, full of the drone of countless insects. There were always clouds of dancing Gnats or Midges, while Bees and Hover Flies darted like small meteors across the sunlit zones, vanishing among the dappled shadows. It was here, on a fallen and rotting Willow trunk, that I first watched a female Greater Horntail, which is a Wood Wasp as large as a Hornet, using her long, saw-like ovipositor to lay her eggs; and here on another occasion I came upon the only Fritillary butterfly – a Pearl-bordered – that I have ever seen in Essex. It was a wood much favoured by Pheasants, which enjoy marshy conditions, and in winter by immigrant Woodcocks; and there was a time – though not in recent years – when I would hardly ever walk through on a summer's day without disturbing a Grass Snake, sunning itself in lazy coils beside the track.

There came a time when the drainage ditches were all dug out, and most of the Alders felled and sold. But many remained, in the more inaccessible parts of the wood, and the felled ones were replaced by hybrid Poplars, so the wood's character did not change dramatically. When I was last there, several years ago, the Alder stubs were producing a very healthy coppice crop, though I doubt if any use will ever be made of it.

I think also of a long row of Alders that grew, not far from this wood, beside a tributary of the river Colne. These had probably been cut over, long ago, to provide poles, for most of them had multiple stems, but they had since grown into large trees. Being open grown, their side branches had spread and they carried, in summer, a mass of dark foliage which was reflected in the water below. On the opposite side of the brook there was an area of damp rough ground, planted with one of the hybrid Poplars – *Populus* 'Robusta' – which, in May, was a sea of creamy-pink Snakeweed flowers. These Alders were worth seeing too, in early spring, when the male catkins hung down like little ropes of garnets from the dark branches which also bore clusters of black, empty seed-cones.

My final picture of Alders comes from a very different setting – a bay at the head of a Highland loch. I was fishing one summer evening at the point where a small burn ran into the loch. Here the Alders were stunted, little bigger than bushes, and their twisted branches were hoary with lichen. They grew from a stony soil, and the gin-clear water of the loch lapped at their roots. I fished on into the dusk, plagued by hordes of Midges, and was forced to wade quite a long way out to be free of them. The scent of Bog Myrtle reached me faintly on the breeze, and I remember looking back to see the silhouettes of the Alders inky black against a sky that shaded upwards from a band of vermilion near the horizon to gold and finally a kind of diluted aquamarine barred by slate-coloured clouds, while high above me, little parties of Mallard and Pintail swept down on set wings towards the reedy shallows of the loch.

THE HORNBEAM

The Hornbeam is native only to south-eastern England and a few parts of the west country and south Wales. Where I live, on the borders of Suffolk and Essex, it occurs occasionally in mixed woodland or as a hedgerow tree, but cannot be described as common.

There was a time when its timber had a number of specialised uses, including flails, ox yokes, cam wheels and butchers' chopping blocks, all of which required exceptionally tough wood; and it was also coppiced extensively for its excellent firewood. Nowadays, however, it is rather a neglected species and except when carrying a good crop of its very distinctive fruits, it is often mistaken for Beech.

Although there are several neighbourhood Hornbeams, with which I am on nodding terms, and one in a nearby wood, with twisting branches and delicate twigs attractive enough to hold my attention for a few minutes when I walk that way in winter, I cannot pretend that the tree has strong associations for me, although I have an early memory of a very handsome Hornbeam hedge in the garden of one of my relations. I also recall that at my cousin's house in Wiltshire, there was a long and gloomy pathway, known as the Major's Walk, leading from the Beech wood above the house down towards the village, which comprised a rather unusual mixture of

HORNBEAM

I

CARPINUS BETULUS

Fig.1

The winter twig of Hornbeam is dark brown, with buds set alternately. The buds, light brown, narrow and pointed, are very similar to those of Beech but differ in that they are closely appressed, while Beech buds project from the twig. Fruit stalks often persist right through the winter.

Fig.2

Buds enlarging and young leaves starting to break out on 17th April.

Fig.3

Flowering twig on 28th April. Female catkins are borne near the tip of the twig and are fairly erect. The slender pink styles emerge from a mass of leafy green bracts. Male catkins are pendulous, with bunches of crimson-anthered stamens protected by yellow-green heart-shaped bracts.

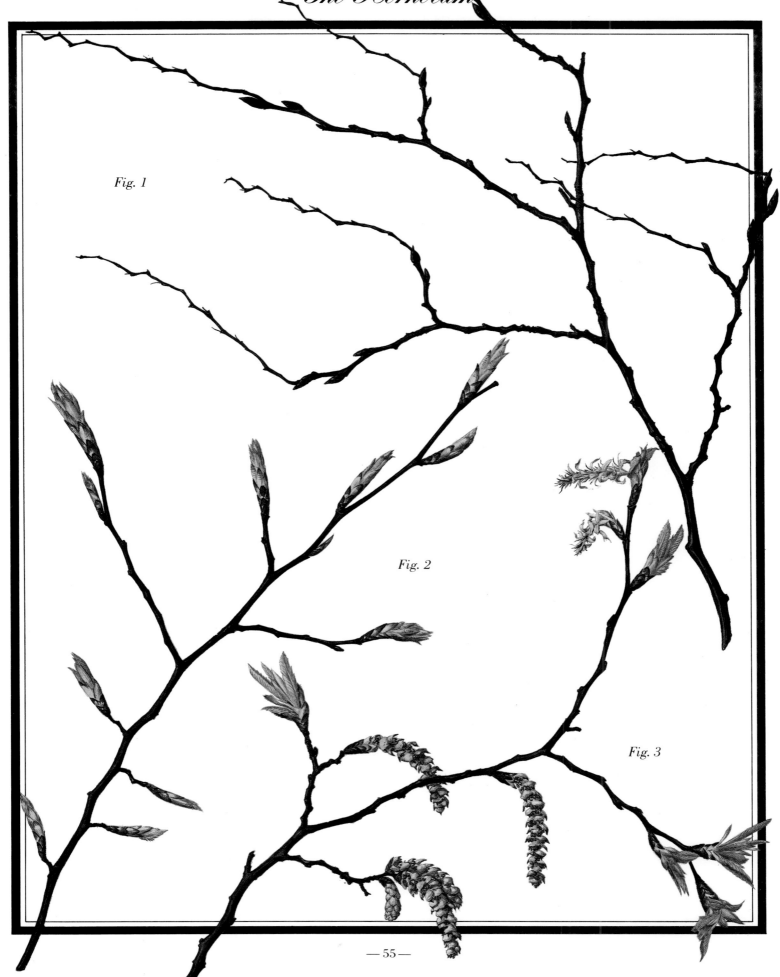

Fig. 1

Fig. 2

Fig. 3

II

Fig. 1

Leaves and fruit on 19th August. The double-toothed leaves are oval with prominent parallel veining, and smooth. The fruits hang down in clusters and consist of opposed pairs of winged seeds. A single such seed is shown at the bottom right of the figure.

Fig. 2

Fruits which have turned a rich golden yellow in October, though the seeds remain green. Such a colour change does not always occur; more often the fruits change gradually from green to brown.

Fig. 3

Autumn leaves on 28th October.

Hornbeam (*Carpinus betulus*).

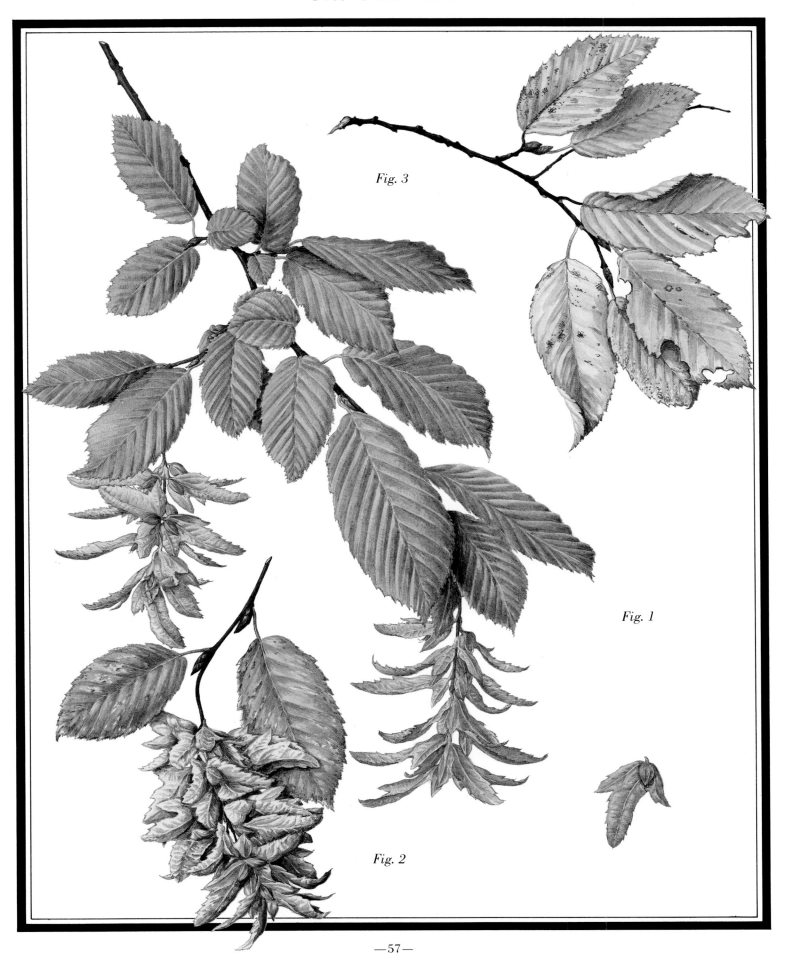

Fig. 3

Fig. 1

Fig. 2

Yews and Hornbeams; but it was a dark, spidery place, and we tended to let the shade of the Major (whoever he was) wander there unchallenged.

Like the Beech, the Hornbeam retains its low-grown leaves through the winter, and since it also coppices well it is an ideal species for hedges. What a pity it is not used more widely in preference to the horrible Leyland Cypress *(Cupressocyparis leylandii),* which has become so prevalent in recent years, bringing an aura of suburbia into many a country garden simply because people lack the patience to plant slower-growing but ultimately much more attractive species.

THE HAZEL

Hazel is to be found in virtually any area of mixed woodlands and well-established hedgerows. Although it barely qualifies as a tree, it is the prime constituent of the underwood where it was once extensively coppiced, and where, even today, it provides useful small timber for the countryman. Beaters cut Hazel sticks for tapping their way through the pheasant coverts, gardeners use it for bean-poles, and the more twiggy parts for pea-sticks, housewives for clothes props; the thatcher still cuts his 'springels' from the Hazel coppice, and there must yet be farmers who choose it for hedge stakes and hurdles. I doubt, though, if anyone nowadays uses Hazel wattles for house-building or Hazel faggots to fuel the bread oven. On my daily walks I see Hazels growing everywhere; deep in the woods and about their margins, in the hedgerows around the old gravel pits, beside the river and along the disused railway line. They are so common that, except in the case of a few good nut-bearers, I do not think of them individually, and yet they make their presence felt at all times of the year. In winter woodlands they often provide the earliest foretaste of spring, reacting to any patch of mild weather with splendid optimism by letting down their long, yellow 'lamb's tail' catkins. With bleak months still lying ahead, it is a heartening sight, and from that moment the signs increase – Primroses and Sweet Violets in flower, Elder coming into leaf, Rooks building, Partridges pairing up, and then the first Chiffchaffs and Willow Warblers singing in the spinney. These things make it easier to bear the cutting north-easters, the sleet and rain, even the mud on the track that leads to my house, during the final onslaughts of winter.

Come the spring, and the Hazel puts forth its tufts of downy, pleated leaves, adding to the lovely powdering of delicate shades of green that softens the stark outlines of winter and lifts the heart at the time when young lambs are chasing in droves across the meadows and birds are starting to sing in earnest.

By haytime the Hazel bushes have swollen into great leafy mounds and you would need a scythe, a billhook and a great deal of muscle power to cut your way into some of their woodland fastnesses. This is the time when you peer among their branches, appraising the crop of nuts, and wondering if the Squirrels will leave any to ripen in September.

The Hazel is also memorable for its autumn colour. The big round leaves turn yellow and then chestnut-brown, but here and there the leaves of a particular tree – generally the same one each year – will have an admixture of the most delicate pink which gives a shade that is unique to the Hazel, and is one of the most beautiful of the woodland's autumn tints.

Dormouse (*Muscardinus avellanarius*).

THE WILLOWS

Was there ever a book named more aptly than Kenneth Grahame's *The Wind in the Willows*? It evokes such a picture of tranquillity, of flat, well-husbanded land, cattle grazing on lush pastures, slow-moving rivers and stands of waving, blue-green Willows. There are many species and subspecies of Willow that grow wild in these islands, some of them small, creeping shrubs, others quite large bushes; but only two, the Crack Willow and the White Willow, grow into large trees, and these, generally found growing together, are typical of that tranquil scene.

HAZEL

CORYLUS AVELLANA

Fig. 1

Hazel twigs in winter are brown and covered with stiff glandular hairs. The buds, stout, blunt and either green or red-brown, are set alternately.

Fig. 2

Twig on 26th January. The male catkins, which may be green or pinkish-brown, have not yet started to expand.

Fig. 3

On 22nd February, the familiar 'lamb's tails' — the male catkins — have come down and are shedding their pollen. Female flowers consist of small bud-like catkins, from the tips of which protrude bunches of crimson styles.

Fig. 4

Leaves starting to emerge on 11th April.

Fig. 5

Young leaves on 16th April.

Fig. 6

Leaves and fruit and a group of male catkin buds on 28th September. Above is a ripe nut at the same date, below a cluster of nuts enclosed by their leafy bracts on 21st August. The large, rounded leaves are thickly hairy on both sides.

Fig. 7

Leaf on 21st November. Hazel leaves, with their mixtures of greens, yellows, pinks and browns, can be very attractive in the autumn.

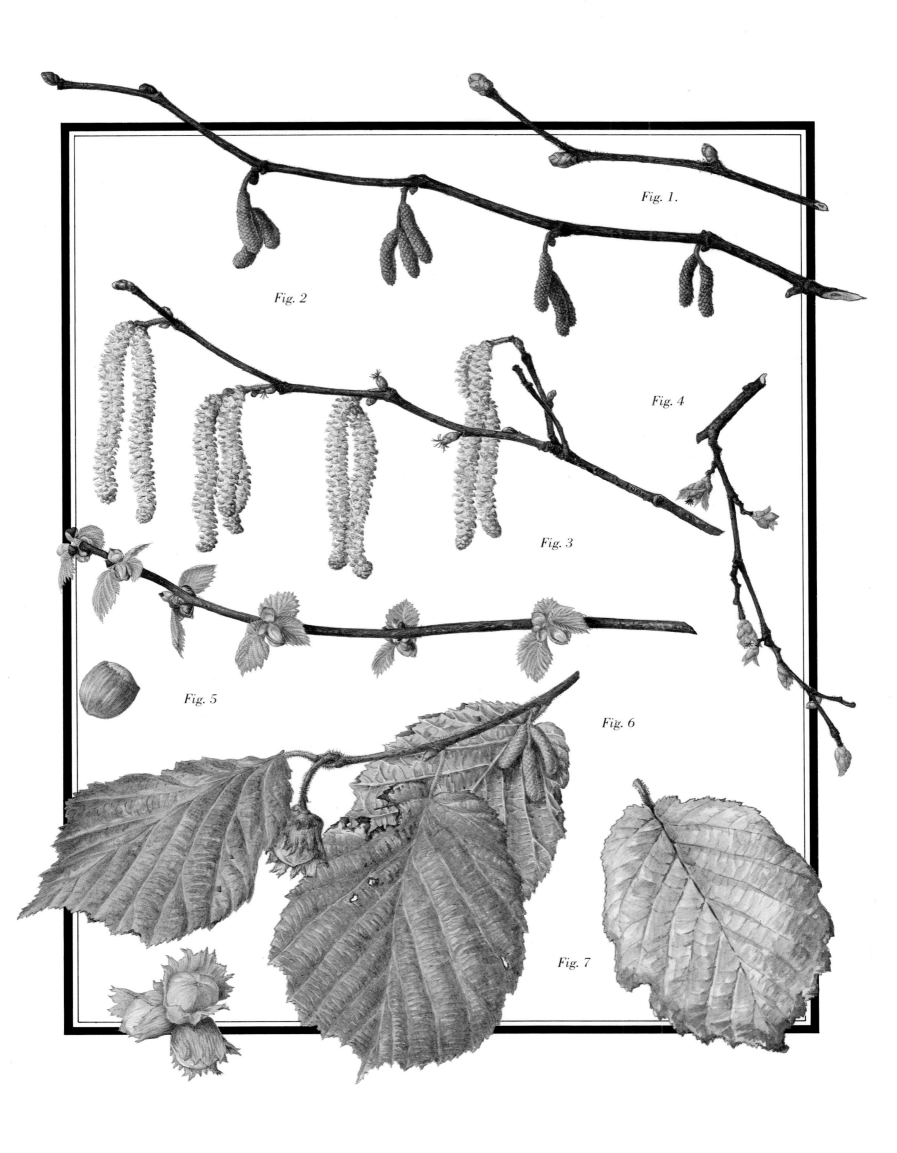

Fig. 1.

Fig. 2

Fig. 4

Fig. 3

Fig. 5

Fig. 6

Fig. 7

WHITE WILLOW
AND VARIETIES

SALIX ALBA

Fig. 1

The small buds are spirally set on the twig and covered with silky white hairs.

Fig. 2

Male catkins on 4th May. They arise on short leafy stalks. The young leaves are downy but do not yet have white undersides.

Fig. 3

Green female catkins, borne on a separate tree to the males.

Fig. 4

Ripe female catkin releasing seed on 24th June.

Fig. 5

Shoot with leaves, mid-August, showing their characteristic white undersides.

Fig. 6

The leaves change colour and fall in sequence, so that the tree does not become yellow all at once.

Fig. 7

Var. *coerulea*, the Cricket-bat Willow. The leaves are bluish-grey on both sides.

Fig. 8

Var. *tristis*, the Weeping Willow. The leaves are brighter green above, grey-green beneath and pendent.

White Willow (*Salix alba*).

Fig. 1

Fig. 2

Fig. 3

Fig. 4

Fig. 5

Fig. 6

Fig. 7

Fig. 8

CRACK WILLOW

SALIX FRAGILIS

Fig. 1

The twig varies from golden to brownish-green, and carries appressed yellowish-brown buds with long, tapering points.

Fig. 2

The young leaves are at first entire and fringed with silky hairs, which soon disappear. The female catkins are slightly longer than those of *S. alba*, otherwise very similar at this stage.

Fig. 3

Female catkin, 20th June. Here it can be seen that the capsules are on short stalks, whereas those of *S. alba* are sessile. The lower capsules have turned brown and split open to release their seed.

Fig. 4

Male catkins, beginning of May. They are stouter and silkier than those of *S. alba* and, seen from a distance, a less brilliant yellow.

Fig. 5

The leaves are lanceolate and serrate, up to 6″ in length, and glabrous. They are green above and a slightly greyer shade of green beneath.

Fig. 6

Throughout October, individual leaves turn to a deep, rich yellow before they fall.

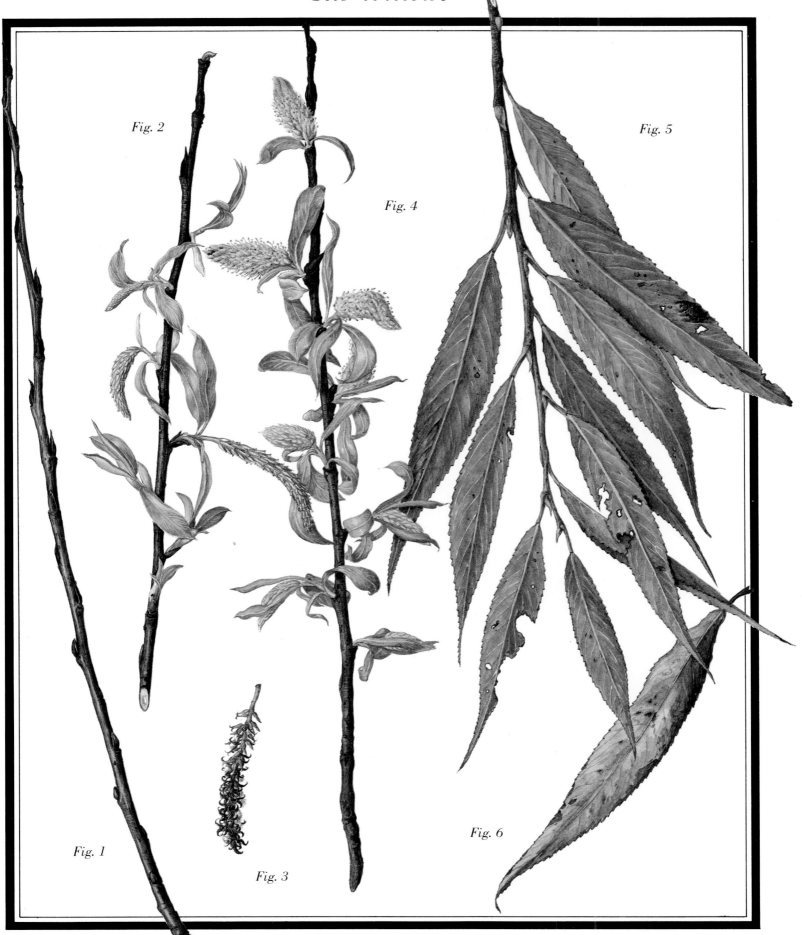

Fig. 2

Fig. 4

Fig. 5

Fig. 1

Fig. 3

Fig. 6

GOAT WILLOW

SALIX CAPREA

Fig. 1

Winter twig in February, bearing large, single-scaled, shiny-brown catkin buds. Twigs may be olive-green, red or purple.

Fig. 2

Winter twig bearing only the smaller growth buds.

Fig. 3

Twig in early March, with silky white catkins starting to emerge.

Fig. 4

Male flowers producing pollen on 4th April.

Fig. 5

Twig with greenish-yellow female catkins on 14th April. As with all Willows, male and female flowers are borne on separate trees.

Fig. 6

Ripening fruit on 6th May. By early May young leaves are out all over male trees, on female trees only at tips of twigs.

Fig. 7

Leaves of Goat Willow on 25th September. These are typical, but there can be considerable variation in leaf shape; note pinkish midribs.

Fig. 8

Underside of leaf which is covered by a grey-green pubescence.

Purple Emperor Butterfly (*Apatura iris*).

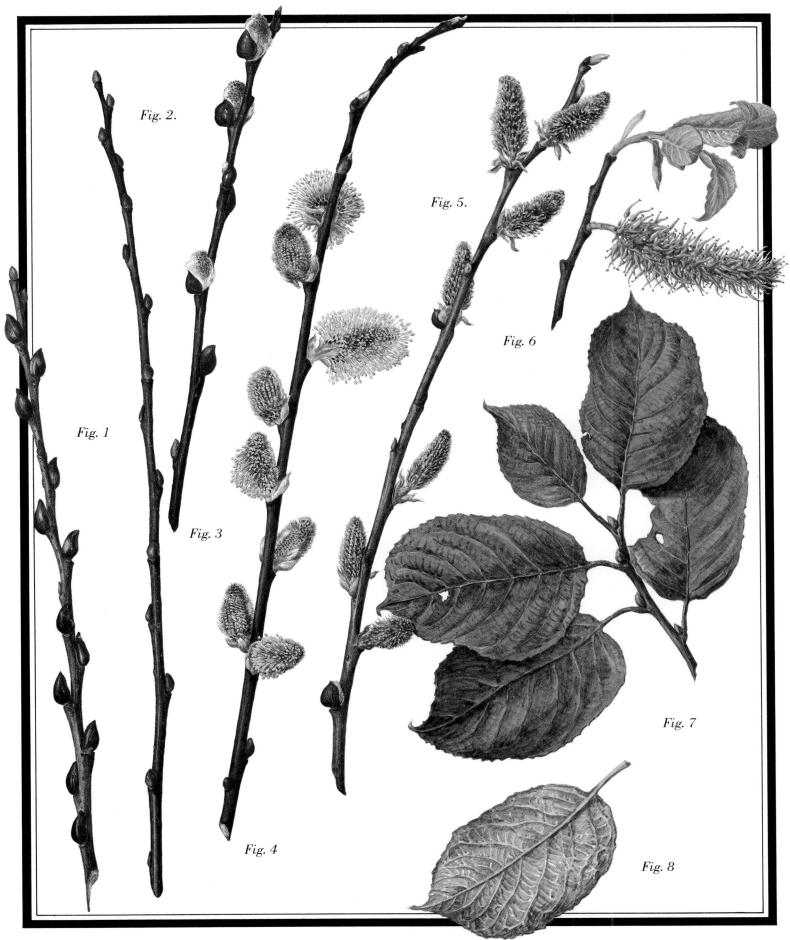

Fig. 1

Fig. 2.

Fig. 3

Fig. 4

Fig. 5.

Fig. 6

Fig. 7

Fig. 8

I live in a village enclosed by a wide bend of the River Stour which here, and for much of its length, forms the boundary between the counties of Suffolk and Essex. All along its valley, Willows grow in profusion, and when the wind blows the White Willows turn up their leaves, showing their white undersides, and appear, from a distance, like rippling silver wave-crests. Many of them stand right at the river's edge, and beneath their trembling curtains of foliage, in summer, the fishermen sit watching their bobbing floats. No doubt they sometimes catch the big silver Bream, the red-finned Roach, the striped Perch and the baleful, predatory Pike that patrol the river's murky depths, but, strangely, they are never seen to do so. And what matter ? With all the world in turmoil, how better to pass time than dream away the idle summer hours amidst the Loosestrife and the Butterburr? When, in my youth, I did quite a lot of coarse fishing, its charm consisted chiefly of such things as sunlight on slow-moving water and the shadows cast by leaf-heavy Oaks and Willows, the 'krek' of a Moorhen threading its way among the Reedmace, the crunching sounds of grazing cattle knee-deep in a Buttercup sward, the soporific hum of a myriad questing insects, the roar of water over a weir, the dark shadows and dancing reflections under the arches of a bridge, and the river's oozy smell mingling with the heavy scent of Meadowsweet.

In winter, when the trees are bare of leaves, the cattle shut up in warm, covered yards, and the tussocky grass and skeletal stems of reed and Hemlock rimed with frost, the river becomes a lonelier place, though still visited by the more intrepid of the fishermen. Then, when the wind blows, and the Willows bend their tawny crests, branches are often reft from the trees, and twigs, particularly the fragile twigs of Crack Willow, are carried by the wind, and then by the river, until they lodge on some muddy bank where they can put down roots and grow, in time, into new trees. No species grows so readily from cuttings as the Willows, as can be confirmed by anyone who has ever tried using the wood for fencing stakes. Unless completely dried out, they will quickly strike root and before long your fence will start sprouting green shoots.

Besides the type, two varieties of White Willow are very commonly encountered and I have included drawings of their leaves on the White Willow plate. The Cricket-bat Willow (*Salix alba* var. *coerulea*), often found in small plantations on low-lying ground, particularly in East Anglia, is grown chiefly for the manufacture of cricket-bats. The Weeping Willow (*S. alba* var. *tristis*) is grown mainly for amenity, but is frequently found beside rivers, well beyond the confines of gardens or purposely landscaped areas.

Of the smaller Willows, there are several species, including the Bay Willow (*S. pentandra*), the Almond Willow (*S. triandra*), the Grey Sallow (*S. cinerea*), the Purple Willow (*S. purpurea*) and the Osier (*S. viminalis*) which sometimes grow into small trees, or into bushes so large as to be almost classed as trees; but I have chosen only one, the Goat Willow or Great Sallow (*S. caprea*), to represent this group. Not only is it the best known and most frequent, but in its tree form it probably reaches the greatest height; one, growing by some old gravel pits near my house, measures forty-two feet and has, unusually, a single main stem.

The Goat Willow is familiar to nearly everyone in springtime under the name of 'Pussy Willow' and a fine, albeit bushy, specimen that grew in the village where I used to live, was always known as the 'butterfly tree' because it attracted so many butterflies when in flower. It grew beside a wide, boggy ride that bisected the big Larch wood in front of my house, a favourite haunt of mine on fine days in early spring, and also in late May and June, when the pink and white spikes of Marsh and Spotted Orchid grew in its wetter parts. There were other Sallow bushes growing along the edge of the ride, together with Alders, a few Birches and young Oak trees, and big mounds of Bramble, but the 'butterfly tree', standing on a sunny corner of the Larch plantation, was the largest of the Sallows and always carried a profusion of male flowers. I remember a day in late March, when the temperature was 67°F — very warm for the time of year — and the tree with its mass of ripe, golden catkins had attracted nearly a dozen Small Tortoiseshells and almost as many Commas, besides two or three magnificent Peacocks. Several Brimstones were patrolling up and down the ride, gnats danced in the bright sunshine, Bumblebees and small Mining Bees droned among the pullulating vegetation, and dust motes and Willow pollen swirled and sparkled in the shafts of sunlight that came down through the tops of the Larches. Their bare branches were already powdered with tufts of green needles and the first rosy-pink flowers. The air rang with the sound of birdsong, including the seesaw notes of the Chiffchaff and the liquid, cascading song of the Willow

Warblers, both newly arrived from migration. A Chiffchaff flew into the Willow tree, started to hunt methodically among the branches for insects, and as I watched it through binoculars, I caught a flash of carmine from the Larches beyond, and at the same time heard a high-pitched, rapidly repeated call, which was sufficiently unfamiliar to make me search vigorously among the trees for its originator. After a frustrating ten minutes or so, during which I caught repeated glimpses of small brown birds flitting among the shadows, I managed to get a good view of one, confirming my suspicion that they were Redpolls. It turned out to be quite a large flock of both Redpolls and Siskins, several of which flew into the Willow tree, giving me a chance to study them in detail and make some sketches. In subsequent years I never failed to find them, each spring, in the same locality. I always hoped that some of the Redpolls might stay and nest, for the habitat was ideal, but I never had any evidence that they did so.

Crack Willow (*Salix fragilis*).

THE POPLARS

The Lombardy Poplar, with its tall, columnar outline, is familiar to most people since it is widely planted, but the native Black Poplar, of which it is a variety, is not so well known, and indeed has become, in recent years, an increasingly rare tree as old specimens are dying and modern hybrids are preferred for planting. A fine old Black Poplar grows on the farm of some friends in a neighbouring village. It must be well over a hundred feet high and its remaining branches, as well as its bole, are knobbly with burrs. It stands at the junction of a small brook and a bridleway that runs between large hedgerows, and it towers majestically over all its neighbours. A narrow valley of meadowland, enclosed by thick, tree-lined hedges, follows the course of the brook, constituting an oasis of greenery in a countryside now almost entirely devoted to intensive cereal growing. The meadows are normally grazed only by horses and produce generous crops of Field Mushrooms each autumn. Beside the brook there are boggy patches where Yellow Flag, Marsh Orchid and Ragged Robin grow, and dense thickets of Blackthorn where Badgers have their sets. There are woods also, full of Crack Willow and Alder, and on the northern flank of the valley a sunken bridleway runs between great rampant hedges from which arise mature Oaks and Ashes (the Elms are mostly dead or dying). The ancient origin of the hedges is indicated by the great variety of species found in them, including Spindleberry and Buckthorn, besides the commoner Bramble, Dog Rose, Field Maple, Privet, Quickthorn and the like.

Much more common than the Black Poplar are the hybrid Black Poplars which arose from crossings between *Populus nigra* and various American species, and which are to be found, often in regimented groups, in river valleys, on roadsides, beside railway lines and grown as shelter belts throughout most of lowland Britain. The oldest of these hybrids, and the one most likely to be found in more natural situations — growing, for instance, beside rivers among White and Crack Willows — is the Black Italian Poplar (*P. serotina*), which I have illustrated to represent the group. With its not very numerous, upswept branches and open, rather unbalanced crown, it is easily recognised, always reminding me of a huge twig stuck at random in the ground. In some wet meadows where I used often to walk my dogs, there were

BLACK POPLAR

POPULUS NIGRA

Fig. 1

Winter twig of Black Poplar: typically pale ochreous brown – with its glossy brown, pointed, spirally arranged buds. These are flower buds and project slightly from the stem. Leaf buds (one at base and several near apex of twig) are smaller, and closely appressed.

Fig. 2

Black Poplar twig, bearing pale yellowish-green female catkins, at the end of March. The terminal bud is starting to swell and will produce a leafy shoot. Above the twig is a female catkin drawn about ten days later. It has expanded to some 3″, and the shiny green capsules in their pale green stalked cups can now be seen clearly.

Fig. 3

Catkins of the uncommon female form of the Lombardy Poplar emerging during the first week of April.

Fig. 4

The splendid bright crimson male catkins of the Lombardy Poplar starting to expand on 29th March. Male catkins of Black Poplar are identical.

Fig. 5

Young leaves of a Black Poplar.

Fig. 6

Leaves from a Lombardy Poplar in early September. Leaves of Black Poplar and Lombardy Poplar differ from those of hybrid Black Poplars in being diamond-shaped rather than triangular (though this distinction is not always very clear), and tend to be smaller.

Fig. 7

Yellow autumn leaf of Black Poplar at the end of September.

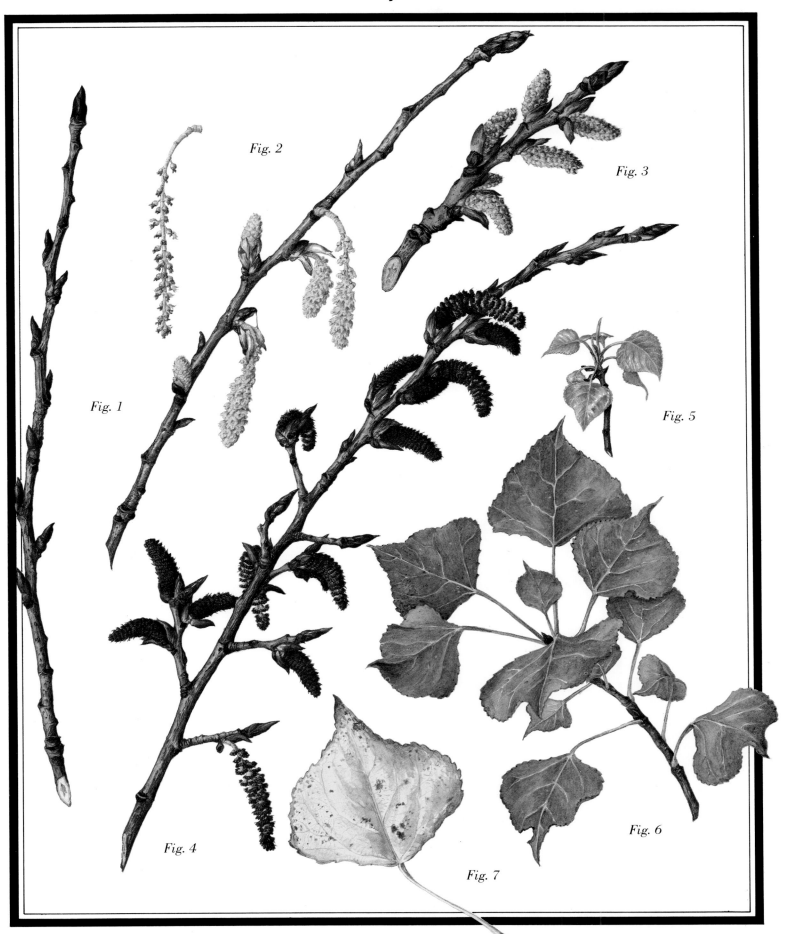

Fig. 1

Fig. 2

Fig. 3

Fig. 4

Fig. 5

Fig. 6

Fig. 7

BLACK ITALIAN POPLAR

POPULUS SEROTINA

Fig. 1

Twig, bearing only leaf and growth buds. These are similar to the flower buds – long, pointed, curving slightly away from the stem – but smaller.

Fig. 2

Another winter twig, this time a stout twig bearing many large flower buds and taken from the very top of the tree. Note the star-shaped pith, which is typical of all the Poplar family.

Fig. 3

P. serotina produces only male flowers (which means that it does not produce seed and can therefore only be propagated by means of cuttings). Here, the large crimson male catkins are emerging on 23rd April. The terminal bud is a growth bud and will open later to send out a new shoot.

Fig. 4

Young leaves on 20th May.

Fig. 5

Shoot with leaves at the beginning of October. The leaves are larger than those of *P. nigra* and more triangular in shape. The leaf stalk is flattened near the base of the leaf.

Fig. 6

Leaves turning bright yellow in mid-October.

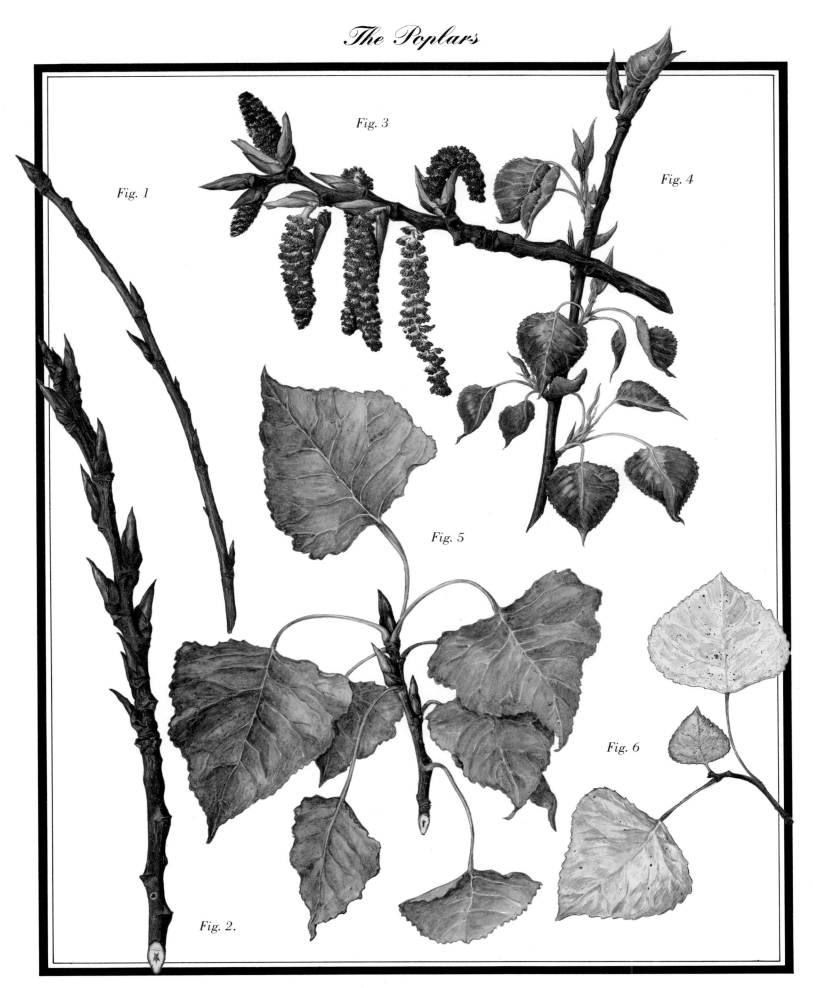

Fig. 1

Fig. 3

Fig. 4

Fig. 5

Fig. 6

Fig. 2.

several fine specimens of Black Italian Poplar growing alongside the river and beside the drainage ditches that fed into it at intervals. During the winter, the meadows always held Snipe, which would rise, singly or in pairs, in front of the dogs with harsh, scraping cries and zigzag flight.

As open-grown mature trees, White and Grey Poplars differ considerably in form, but in other respects, and when grown close together, they are sufficiently similar to cause confusion, especially at those times of year when there are no leaves. White Poplars are at their best in summer on a breezy, sunny day when gusts of wind expose the brilliant white undersides of their leaves. I think of them, on such a day, growing in the valley of the River Waveney on the Suffolk-Norfolk border – not, for the most part, large trees, but clumps of vigorous sucker growth, that bend together with the wind and turn, as if by magic, from green to silvery-white and back again to green.

Grey Poplars are in this respect less spectacular, since the undersides of their leaves are grey rather than white and are only noticeable in early summer; but they grow to a greater size, and old specimens can make very handsome park trees. I had to travel down to Surrey in order to make my drawing of the winter tree, since in my neighbourhood I could find clumps or groves of Grey Poplars – one beside the river in my own village – but no specimen trees.

Black Italian Poplar (*Populus serotina*).

Black Poplar (*Populus nigra*).

The Aspen gave me similar problems. I knew of just one wood where Aspens grew, and these provided me with the specimens for the colour plate, but I could find no open-grown trees, and it was not until a few years ago, when I was fishing in September on the Spey, that I first saw really good specimens of Aspen growing in the open. They grew beside the river itself, along with Rowans, Wych Elms, Bird Cherries and Birches, but the best specimens I found were on the wooded slopes of a hill a few miles from the river, where they grew with Silver Birches and old Scots Pines. I was panting my way up a steep track, looking for interesting toadstools and keeping an eye out for Roe deer which would sometimes appear, briefly immobile, with twitching noses and pricked ears, before bounding off into the tall Bracken, when there was a clatter and whirr of wings, and a huge brown bird, which had been perched in a tree high above me, went sailing off over the valley. It was the first Capercaillie I had ever seen, and as I continued my walk, I put up eight more, one after the other. It was while peering up in search of them that I noticed a group of several mature Aspens, some with leaves already turning bright yellow; and later, higher up the slope, I came across others, their leaves fluttering softly in the gentle breeze.

The last of our Poplars, the Balsam Poplar, is an alien of fairly recent introduction, and belongs to one of the confusing groups of trees which, in

ASPEN

POPULUS TREMULA

Fig. 1

Winter twig on 1st February, showing growth buds and two of the much fatter flower buds.

Fig. 2

Winter twig showing only growth buds which are long, pointed, shiny brown and appressed.

Fig. 3

Twig with hairy female catkins on 9th February.

Fig. 4

Male catkins on about the same date. They are larger and very handsome with deep crimson anthers and long chocolate-brown hairs on the bracts.

Fig. 5

Fruiting catkin shedding woolly seeds on 14th May.

Fig. 6

Leafy shoot on 26th September. The leaves are round, with wavy margins and long, flattened petioles which give them their continual fluttering motion.

Fig. 7

Autumn colour can be very fine. These leaves from an Essex tree (15th October) show a variety of rich colours; trees that I saw this year on Speyside, however, were all yellow.

Aspen (*Populus tremula*).

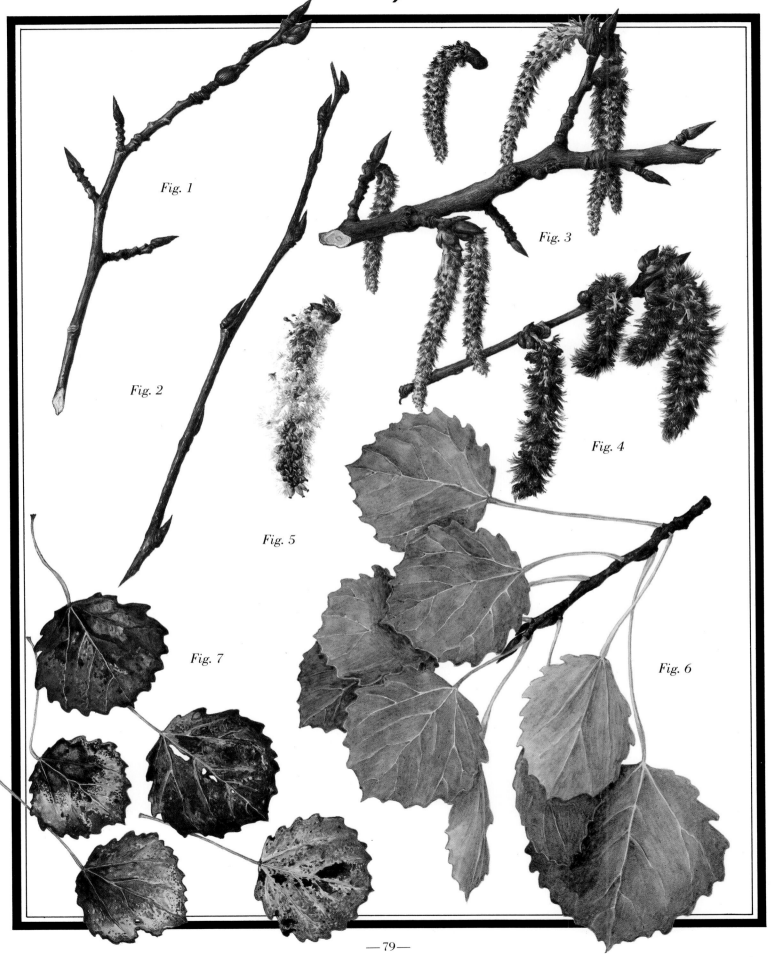

Fig. 1

Fig. 2

Fig. 3

Fig. 4

Fig. 5

Fig. 6

Fig. 7

WHITE POPLAR

POPULUS ALBA

Fig. 1

The winter twig is brown, covered with white pubescence. Buds are in a spiral: plump, pointed, pale brown with white pubescence.

Fig. 2

Female catkins emerging on 27th March. Male catkins (very uncommon and not illustrated here) have crimson anthers and grey hairy bracts.

Fig. 3

Female catkins and swelling leaf buds on 9th April.

Fig. 4

Young leaves on 26th April. Green and mealy on upper surfaces, covered with dense white pubescence on undersides.

Fig. 5

Leaves from the crown of a mature tree on 18th May, and ripe catkins starting to shed seed.

Fig. 6

Leaves, still covered with dense pubescence on their undersides, now much darker green above, at the end of September. These leaves, much more sharply lobed than those in Fig. 5, come from vigorous sucker shoots such as are often found growing at the base of a mature tree.

Fig. 7

Autumn leaf on 15th October.

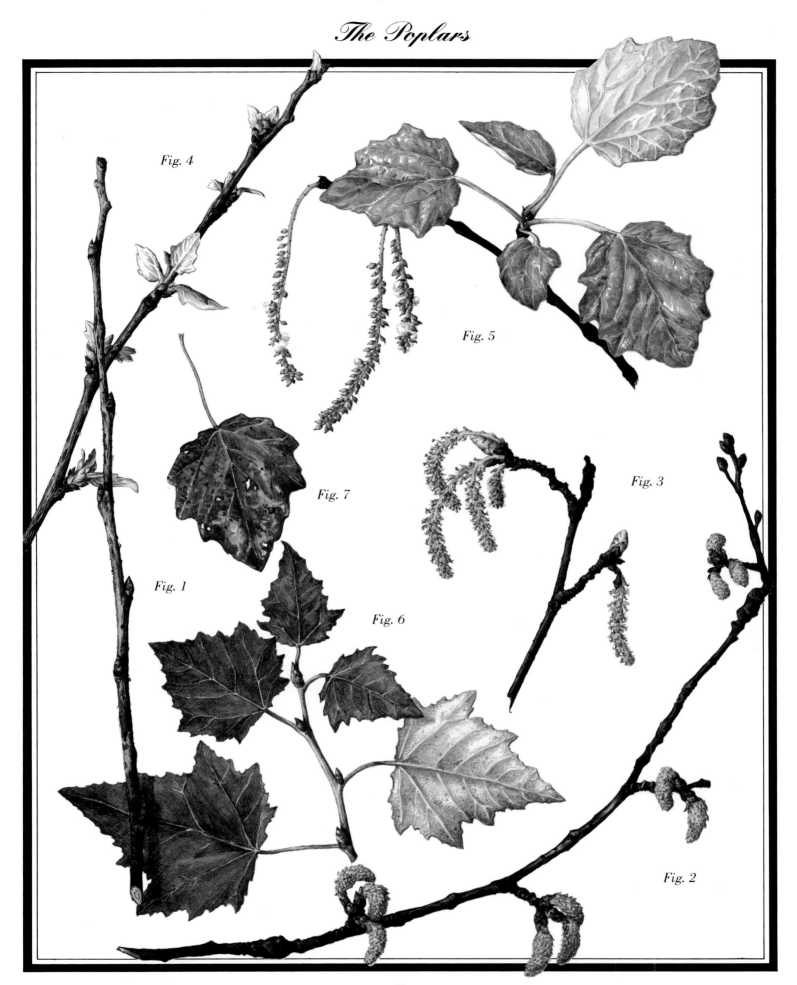

Fig. 4

Fig. 5

Fig. 7

Fig. 3

Fig. 1

Fig. 6

Fig. 2

GREY POPLAR

POPULUS CANESCENS

Fig. 1

The twig in winter is brown with a very short dirty grey pubescence, which can be rubbed off with a finger. The buds are squat, pointed, chestnut-brown with a greyish pubescence, and project hardly at all from the twig.

Fig. 2

A twig furnished with male catkins on 18th March. The anthers progress from orange to crimson, and each flower has a hairy purplish-brown bract.

Fig. 3

Female catkins (which are very rare in Britain, through frequent on the Continent) in early April. The capsules will later release a mass of fluffy seeds.

Fig. 4

Young leaves on 20th May. At this stage their undersides are very white and there is little to differentiate them from the leaves of White Poplar. Leaves from vigorous young trees and sucker shoots may be distinctly lobed, with white-felted undersides, virtually indistinguishable from White Poplar.

Fig. 5

Leaves of Grey Poplar on 16th August. They are intermediate in shape between the leaves of Aspen and White Poplar, but are variable; a surer guide is the greyish rather than white pubescence on their undersides, which may have disappeared by the end of the summer.

Fig. 6

Autumn leaves, like those of other members of this group of Poplars, become blotched with a variety of colours.

Grey Poplar (*Populus canescens*).

Fig. 4

Fig. 2

Fig. 1

Fig. 3

Fig. 5

Fig. 6

BALSAM POPLAR

POPULUS GILEADENSIS

Fig.1

The twigs are stout, grey-brown; the newer wood bearing the buds is dark glossy brown with short bristly hairs. Flower buds are borne throughout the tree and are large, pointed, sticky and scented.

Fig.2

Female catkins emerging in early April – at this stage of the year the scent from the trees is strongest. I have never found male catkins and I understand that they do not occur, or are very rare, in this country.

Fig.3

Fully expanded catkin, showing more clearly the curiously lobed stigmas arising from dark green ovaries contained in pale green cups.

Fig.4

Young leaves emerging and unrolling in late April.

Fig.5

Leaves and fruit on 12th May. The leaves are heart-shaped with serrate edges and have hairy, rounded petioles; at this stage they are bright yellowish-green, grey-green on the undersides. The shiny green capsules will later split open to release masses of white cottonwool-like down.

Fig.6

Leaf in late summer, now darker green above and whiter beneath.

Fig.7

In autumn, the leaf may become a rich, deep yellow, though often it is simply a darker and dingier shade of green.

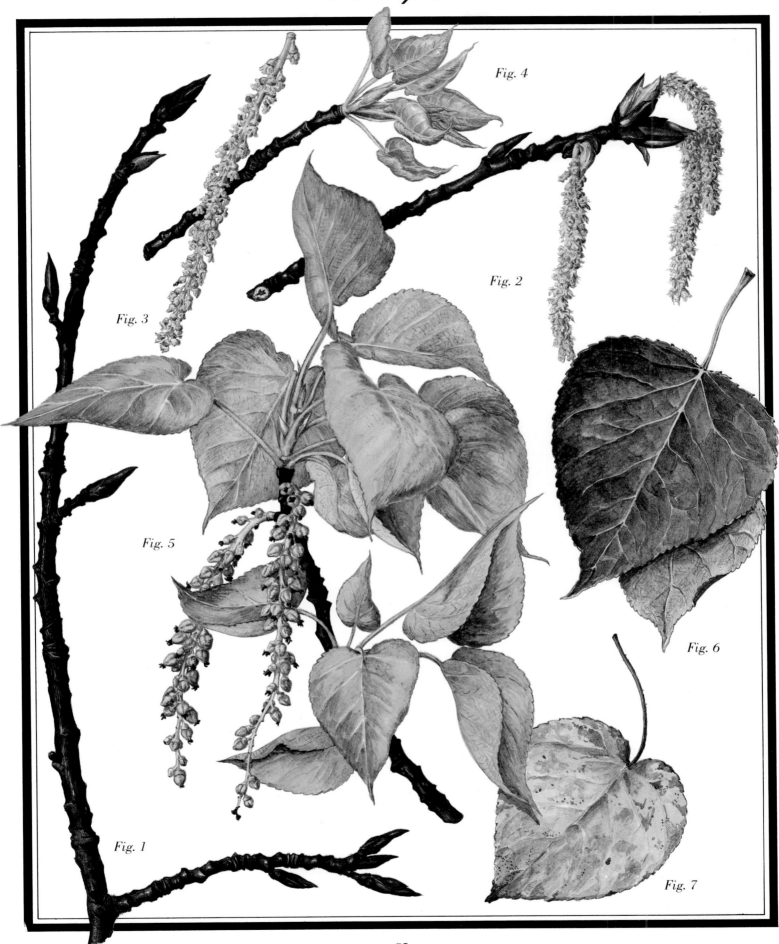

Fig. 4

Fig. 2

Fig. 3

Fig. 5

Fig. 6

Fig. 1

Fig. 7

both popular text books and more scholarly works, seem to provoke contradictions when it comes to describing and naming different species and hybrids. A few of these have become well established on suitable sites, particularly in the west of Britain. All give out a strong fragrance, most noticeable in the spring, and as I walked one day beside the River Colne (on the same water meadows where I had found specimens of Black Italian Poplars), it was this exotic scent that first attracted me to the group of Balsam Poplars which I used for my 'winter tree' drawing (page 175). The younger trees, on the left, had grown up from sucker shoots, and as I have subsequently come across others growing in an equally natural environment, it seemed to me that they fulfilled the necessary criteria for inclusion in this work.

White Poplar (*Populus alba*).

THE WALNUT

I suppose that the Walnut must be considered primarily as a garden tree, but it will grow quite readily from seed, and no doubt birds or Squirrels, squabbling over booty, are responsible for the odd nut dropped where it can grow up into a woodland or hedgerow tree. I can think of two good-sized Walnut trees growing on the banks of disused railway lines, and possibly these arose from nuts discarded long ago by surfeited passengers. Who knows? Whatever their origin, Walnut trees occur here and there in the countryside, and I am reminded of one that I knew well in my youth.

The spot where it grew was approached by a long sunken track that ran through old Sweet Chestnut coppice. At the end of the track was a small meadow that became a sea of yellow Buttercups each May. In June it would be cut for hay and then a few bullocks, or a couple of barren dairy cows, would be taken down to fatten on the clovery aftermath. On the far side of the meadow was another wood, at the edge of which the Walnut tree grew. Once, long ago, there had been a cottage here, nothing remained of the building but the site was still marked by some persistent and uneradicable patches of nettle. The fence around the wood must have taken in part of the former cottage garden, for besides the Walnut tree there were old Gooseberry and Currant bushes growing inside the wood, and an ancient Apple tree that scattered its small crimson codlins on the meadow every autumn.

Probably the cottage had once been inhabited by a gamekeeper, gamekeepers being a race who like to keep themselves to themselves. At any rate, it must always have been a lonely spot, since the cart-track ended at the meadow and only an overgrown footpath continued on through the next wood. I suppose the farmer came each summer morning to check his cattle, but I never met him there, and only once remember seeing a man with a horse-drawn water-cart filling the stone drinking trough that stood under the eaves of the wood. Otherwise I had the place to myself, unless I went there with my young cousins, and a rather eerie spot it was, as though the people who once lived there had left something of their presence behind. Certainly, when I went there in October, to gather such walnuts as had escaped the depredations of Jays and Squirrels, or in summer, to sit reading for an hour or

WALNUT
I

JUGLANS REGIA

Fig. 1

Winter twig. The buds are positioned in a spiral, blunt, with short, velvety hairs, dark green to black, each one surmounting a large, pale-coloured leaf scar. On the lower part of the twig are two male catkin buds.

Fig. 2

Twig on 6th May, the terminal bud starting to burst (the buds do not swell before bursting). Note, at the cut end of the twig, that the pith consists of a series of thin membranes with a hollow space between each.

Fig. 3

Leaves emerging a few days later. Some of the inner bud scales are in fact embryonic leaves.

Fig. 4

The young crimson leaves on 12th May, curling outwards and downwards, expanding at the same time as both male and female flowers.

Walnut (*Juglans regia*).

Fig. 1

Fig. 3

Fig. 2

Fig. 4

II

Fig.1

Twig on 24th May, with new leaves cut away to expose the pair of female flowers in the centre of the shoot. These consist of green, hairy, flask-shaped ovaries from which emerge minute sepals and crinkled, yellowish-green stigmas. The male flowers consist of long, fat, greenish-yellow catkins which arise from the previous year's wood.

Fig.2

By mid-August, the fruit is fully formed; smooth, oval, pale green speckled with white spots.

Fig.3

Leaf and fruit on 21st September. The leaves are pinnate, the leaflets three to nine in number, sessile, oval and entire; the apical are the largest (up to 10″ long), other pairs gradually diminishing in size. They are smooth, rather leathery in texture, and dull, dark green with yellowish veins. In the autumn, they become darker and blotched before falling, but do not take on any distinctive colouring. Both leaves and fruit are aromatic when rubbed, and their juice will stain fingers brown. By this date, the fleshy cases which contain the seed are starting to crack and wither.

Fig.4

Fallen fruit on 27th September, the green outer husk split open to reveal the familiar walnut with its hard, corrugated, pale brown shell. The main fall occurs from the beginning of October.

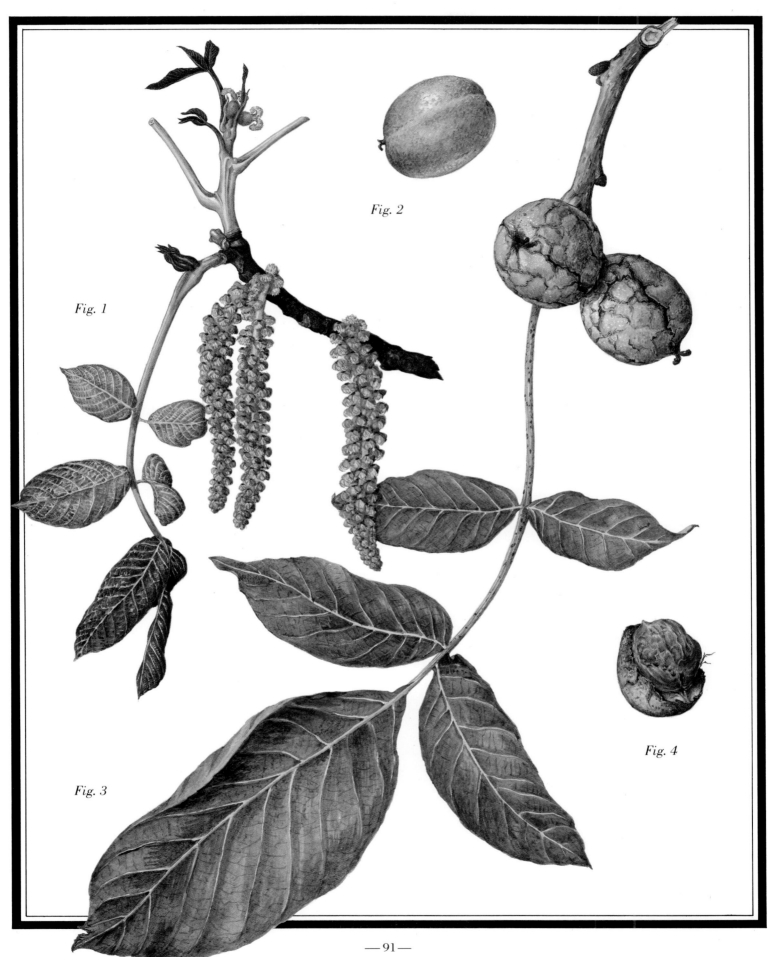

Fig. 1

Fig. 2

Fig. 3

Fig. 4

two with my back against a sweet-scented haycock, I often felt a momentary frisson of discomfort, as though, despite the silence and apparent solitude, unseen eyes were watching me attentively from the bosky shadows beyond the Walnut tree.

THE ELMS

The tragedy of the dead and dying Elms that stand, like gaunt skeletons, throughout the length and breadth of our low-land countryside is heightened by the fact that in recent decades so many trees of all kinds have been destroyed, deliberately or inadvertently, by man. It does seem like a malign act of Providence that such a scourge as Dutch Elm disease should have struck at this precise moment in history.

The younger generations cannot remember the traditional appearance of much of our English countryside, with its distant views of varicoloured fields, all enclosed by stout, stock-proof hedges from which grew countless trees, many of them Elms. Their crowns rose up in summer like banks of billowing cumulus between the cornfields and the meadows, line after line of them, their undulating crests fading into blue distances. This was the famous patchwork landscape extolled by poets, reproduced by countless painters, and which inspired some of the most quintessentially English music. Now much of it has gone, and in its place are arable prairies over which the never-idle sprayer pours out a continuous stream of noxious liquids while the soil's fertility, built up by generations of patient husbandry, imperceptibly leaches away.

In that old farming landscape, the Elm was king: the English Elm throughout most of midland and southern England, the Smooth-leaved Elm in East Anglia and the Cornish Elm in the far west. In the Vale of Avon, where I spent much of my boyhood, English Elms grew in serried ranks from every hedgerow. There were Willows along the watercourses and the

Elm bark with larval feeding galleries of the Elm Bark Beetle
(*Scolytus scolytus*).

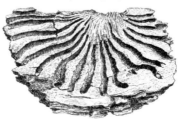

occasional Oak, Ash and other trees, but Elms dominated the scene, and when the disease struck, the devastation was terrible. I remember looking out over the vale some years ago, and being reminded of pictures I had seen of First-World-War battlefields after weeks of continuous shelling.

The English Elm was also the dominant tree, though less exclusively so, on the Oxfordshire farm where I worked for a year as a student back in the early 1950s, in Gloucestershire, where I spent the next three years at agricultural college, and in Leicestershire, where I lived for a year shortly afterwards. Of all trees, it is the one that I associate most closely with the farming scene, being so essentially a tree of the hedgerow, and it forms the background to innumerable vignettes recalled from those days.

The Elms, indeed, witnessed the very end of an era. Before they started to die in their thousands, they saw the last working horses pensioned off, or sent to the knacker's yard, the last wheat sheaves carted to the rick-yard, the last root fields hoed by hand and the last ricks and barns thatched.

I can still see the Elms now on a crisp winter's morning, standing in groups around the farmyard, the fine tracery of their crowns silhouetted in sepia against the pallid sky. In the yard all was bustle and activity as the threshing tackle lumbered, puffing and clanking, into position, and the first of the corn ricks — its protective thatch ripped off — yielded up its golden sheaves into the voracious maw of the machine. The steam engine that drove the tackle belched out black smoke that mixed with the thick dust rising from the threshing drum until the outlines of the Elms were swimming in a murky haze, and chaff and wisps of straw, floating up into the air, blew away high over the tops of the buildings. Men were everywhere, for all hands were pressed into service at threshing time; some with pitchforks on the corn rick, others on the box to catch the sheaves, cut the strings, and feed them into the machine. At one end of the tackle, the threshed straw was disgorged, and another man forked it into a stationary baler which in turn coughed out heavy, wire-bound bales. These were loaded onto an elevator, and as the wheat rick diminished, so the great edifice of straw bales rose up. At the other end of the tackle, the grain was sacked off, and the huge, unwieldy sacks — a sack or coomb of wheat weighed two and a quarter hundredweights — were trundled off on barrows and stacked two-high in the barn. Meanwhile, between these two operations, boys had the dirtiest job of all: carting away the chaff in thin hessian bags to be used as feed, and the cavings – broken straw, empty ears and rubbish – to be spread in the sheepcote as litter. And all the time the foreman would be moving from one part of the operation to another, checking that all was going smoothly, while his terrier, in a frenzy of excitement, rushed round and round the base of the wheat rick, ready for the first rat to bolt.

By the end of March, as the lambing fold rang with the anxious bleats of new-born lambs, and the tractors went jolting over the ploughed fields, pulling down the ridges in readiness for the spring sowing, the Elms took on a purplish haze, indicating that the little cushions of crimson flowers on their slender twigs were in bloom; and in May, with the Cuckoo arrived and the spring corn all drilled, harrowed in and rolled down smooth as ridged sand on the seashore, they would be mantled in the palest shades of saffron and lime-green as the clusters of papery fruits mingled with newly emerged leaves.

Come haytime, all the trees were arrayed in their full panoply of fresh, bright green leaves. How splendid the English Elms were then, rearing up out of the hedgerows with their broad, billowing crowns and narrower skirts of dense foliage.

In the meadows watched over by the Elms, the mower sliced through the stands of tall grass, leaving neat swathes on the ground while clouds of yellow pollen hung on the air behind it; and some days later, if the weather held, the swathe-turner and the tedder would follow on, turning and tossing the hay until the rows lay deep and feathery-light, blue-green and sweetly scented, ready to be put into cocks and then carried, on wooden-tined sweeps, into the rick-yard.

During their dinner hour, the men sat or lay beside the hedge to eat their sandwiches and drink their cold tea under the leafy shade of the Elms, while Woodpigeons cooed and insects droned and the Elm leaves murmured in the breeze.

Between haymaking and harvest, the leaves of the Elm trees darkened. By the time the stooked sheaves were set out across the stubbles and the heaped wagons were trundling back and forth between field and yard, the hedgerows and the trees growing from them formed friezes that seemed almost black against the sky. How clearly I can see the vivid cobalt of those

August skies, with great cumulus clouds, like the hulls of huge white ships, sailing across them, sending their purple shadows racing over the red-gold stubble fields. The cries of the harvesters, as they tossed the sheaves up to the loaders on the wagons, and the shouts of the boys, waiting with sticks around the standing corn for bolting rabbits, still echo in my ears. In my earliest memories of harvest, there is the creak of painted wagon wheels, the jingle of harness, and — most unforgettable of all — the sight and smell of the great, sweating Shire horses that worked so patiently all through those long, hot summer days.

The Elms preside, in my mind, over these and countless other scenes of the farming year; and when autumn came, with its riotous skies and magnificent sunsets, the Elms turned brilliant yellow and gold and formed the background to yet another phase in that endless cycle, as the plough-shares bit into the stubbles and turned over the rich dark earth in shiny ridges, while the seagulls clamoured at the plough-tail, and swooped on any succulent morsels exposed by the gleaming mouldboards.

English Elm (*Ulmus procera*).

ENGLISH ELM

ULMUS PROCERA

Fig. 1

Pale brown winter twig with its very small oval growth buds and larger, rounded flower buds, arranged alternately. Twigs and buds are hairy.

Fig. 2

Flowering twig on 4th April.

Fig. 3

Swelling growth buds on 22nd April.

Fig. 4

Fruiting twig on 3rd May. Elm fruits consist of papery wings or 'samaras', with a single seed placed more or less centrally; these are important in identifying species. The fruit of English Elm is small, round and has the seed placed near the apical notch.

Fig. 5

Young leaves on 5th May.

Fig. 6

Summer leaves. They are more rounded than those on any other Elm, dark green, with rough hairs on the upper surface, and are unequal at the base.

Fig. 7

Golden-yellow autumn leaf on 20th November.

Volvariella bombycina. A fungus which grows from dead wood, particularly Elm.

Fig. 1

Fig. 2

Fig. 4

Fig. 3

Fig. 6

Fig. 5

Fig. 7

SMOOTH LEAVED ELM

ULMUS CARPINIFOLIA

Fig. 1

Winter twig with flower buds and growth buds on 14th February. It is glabrous, though the buds are pubescent.

Fig. 2

Flowering twig on 2nd April.

Fig. 3

Fruiting twig on 4th May. The fruits are oval or obovate, with the seed placed close to the apical notch.

Fig. 4

Bud-burst on 9th May.

Fig. 5

Leafy twig in late summer. The leaves are longer and more sharply pointed than those of English Elm, and are smooth on both surfaces. They are very unequal at the base.

Fig. 6

Autumn leaves on 11th November. The lower example is from a hybrid or variety, and is *not* typical.

Smooth-leaved Elm (*Ulmus carpinifolia*).

The Elms

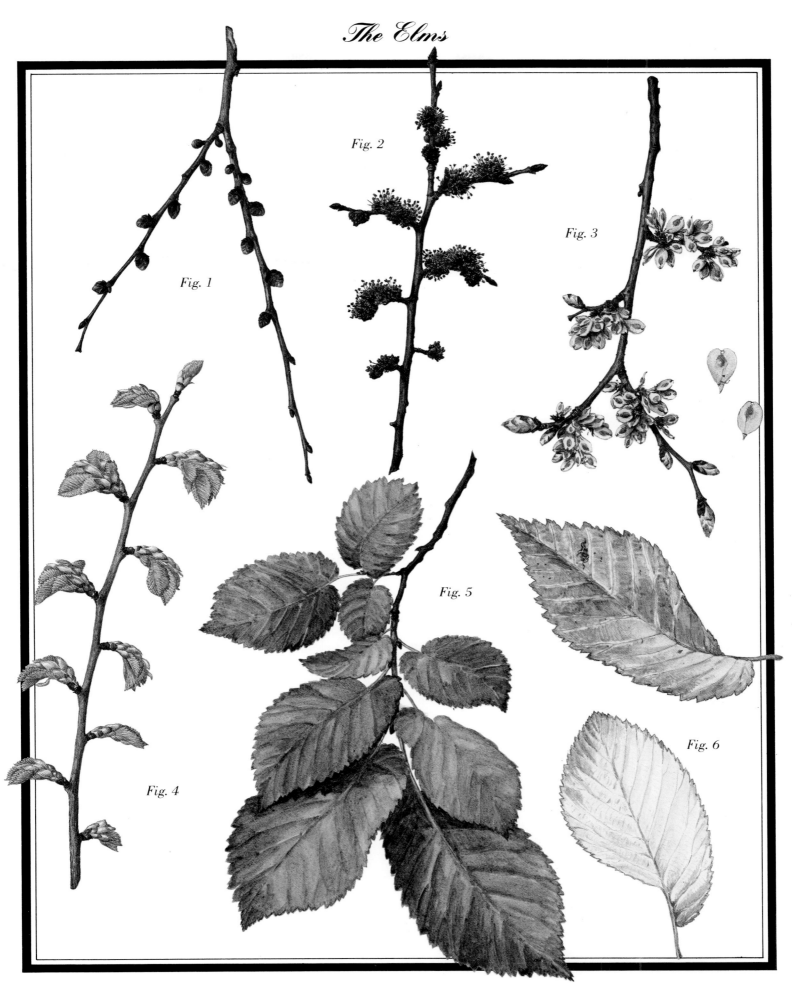

Fig. 1

Fig. 2

Fig. 3

Fig. 4

Fig. 5

Fig. 6

WYCH ELM

ULMUS GLABRA

Fig. 1

Winter twig of Wych Elm: stout and dark-coloured with a close pubescence. Its buds are also large, the flower buds dark brown, the growth buds almost black.

Fig. 2

Flowering twig in late March.

Fig. 3

Fruiting twig on 1st May. The fruits are larger than those of the Field Elms and have the seed cavity placed centrally.

Fig. 4

Buds bursting on 11th May.

Fig. 5

Leaves of Wych Elm are large, varying from 3″ to 6″, and are rough on both surfaces. The base of the longer side is rounded, hiding the very short petiole. The apex of the leaf is extended into a long narrow point, and there may be, as in this example, pointed lobes on either side of the apex, though in Britain this feature is more often found on sucker shoots than on mature trees.

Fig. 6

Autumn leaf on 11th November, showing typical shape for British trees.

Wych Elm (*Ulmus glabra*).

Fig. 1

Fig. 2

Fig. 3

Fig. 4

Fig. 5

Fig. 6

DUTCH ELM

ULMUS X HOLLANDICA

Fig.1

Winter twig in February.

Fig.2

Flowering twig in early April.

Fig.3

Fruiting twig on 8th May. The fruits tend to be very large and the seed cavity is placed half-way between the central point and the apical notch.

Fig.4

Young leaves emerging on 5th May.

Fig.5

Leaves of Dutch Elm are large and may be smooth or slightly hairy on the upper surface. They differ from those of Wych Elm in having long petioles, which are *not* covered by the base of the longer side of the leaf.

Fig.6

Pale gold autumn leaf on 25th September.

Dutch Elm (*Ulmus* x *hollandica*).

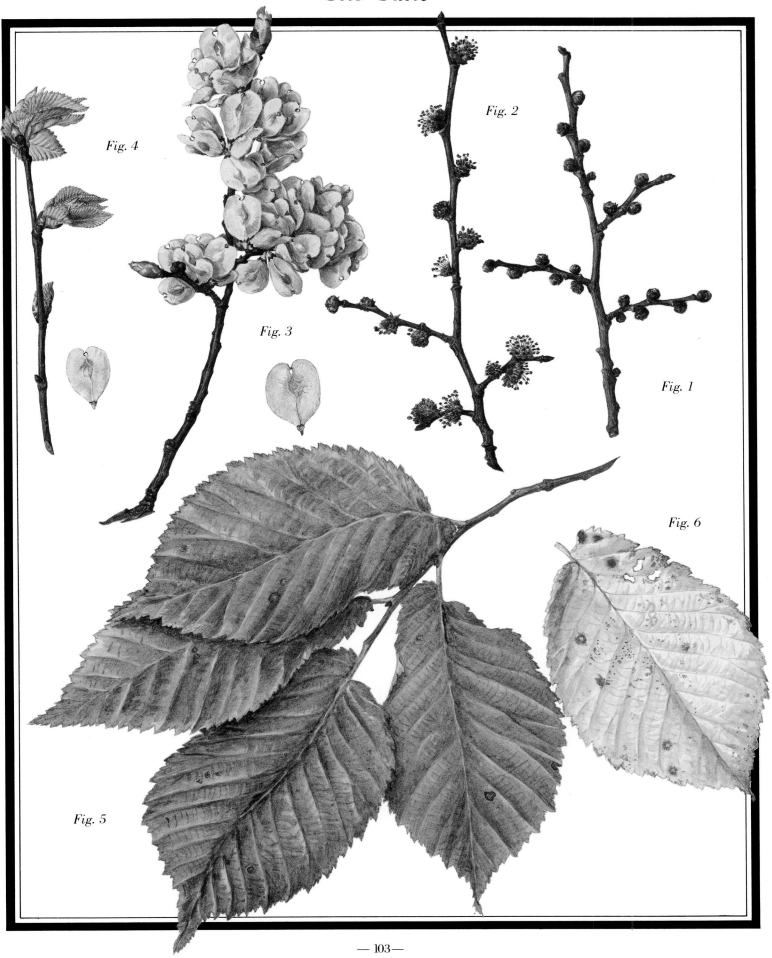

Fig. 4

Fig. 2

Fig. 3

Fig. 1

Fig. 6

Fig. 5

In north Essex, where from 1959 I was to live and farm for more than twenty years, the English Elms were few and far between, and I doubt if any are now left, for they were the first to fall victim to the disease. Their place in the hedgerow was taken by the Smooth-leaved Elm, together with a bewildering selection of hybrids and varieties. Many of these trees, through long associations, I came to know as individuals, and to mourn as such when the disease claimed them.

The typical Smooth-leaved Elm is a tall, narrowly domed tree, with long ascending and arching branches, and pendulous shoots, It always has hairless leaves, but many of the trees in my area lacked pendent shoots and there was considerable variation in shape, in leaf size and in minor details such as colour of the fruits. More commonly than the English Elm, it was a woodland tree, and was the chief constituent of many of the small woods in the district. Even now, as I sit at my desk, I can look out of the window at still-healthy Smooth-leaved Elms, mixed with Oaks, in the small spinney opposite my house. But there are dead trees there as well, and I wonder for how many more summers I will find, as I did last July, a White Letter Hairstreak butterfly in my garden, for this is a species whose only larval food-plant is the Elm, so that their survival is directly linked with that of the tree.

During those farming years in Essex, I could find, within half a mile of my house, the four main species of Elm that I have illustrated, as well as the Huntingdon Elm, which is a variety of Dutch Elm, and the Plot Elm, a variety of Smooth-leaved Elm (another being the Cornish Elm, which is the predominant species in Cornwall and parts of Devonshire).

In particular, there was a very fine old Dutch Elm within fifty yards of my house (I counted 217 annual rings when it eventually had to be felled), and on the neighbouring farm a row of splendid Wych Elms — still, when I last saw them, apparently healthy.

The Wych Elm, however, is one species that I associate as much, or more, with upland scenery, as with the lowland, farming landscape. In Scotland, it is frequently a riverside tree, and I have one fond memory of a highland stream, with Wych Elms growing on the further bank, and behind them a montage of mountain peaks fading from purple to vitreous blue. I sat on a rock a little way back from the water, waiting for the sun to set before starting to fish for Sea Trout. The pool in front of me was inky black from the reflections of the Elms, but every now and then a fish would jump, always in the same spot, and the rings that spread out across the surface of the pool were lit by the setting sun, golden at first, then rosy and finally deep violet as dusk gave way to the still luminous northern night.

THE MAPLES

The Essex village where I lived for many years was called Maple-stead, and no doubt the name referred to the Field Maples – our only native species – which still formed a predominant part of many of the hedges in the neighbourhood. Stout little Maple trees grew here and there, in hedgerows, in field corners or at the edges of woods, but as a rule the Maple was just one among the rich diversity of species that made up the older hedges, and was cut back each time the hedge was trimmed or laid. Inconspicuous for most of the year, and often confused, on account of similar leaf-shape, with Hawthorn, it came into its own in the autumn when the leaves turned brilliant yellow and orange.

There are occasional years when, as a result of some inexplicable set of climatic circumstances, these autumn colours go beyond their normal limits and achieve an altogether unusual degree of splendour. I remember one season, almost twenty years ago, when all the Field Maples, particularly those in the hedges, went on from orange to become vivid scarlet and then crimson before falling. It was a truly splendid sight and even their much grander cousins in New England could not have put on a better show.

The Norway Maple, which has been with us for three hundred years without ever spreading very far into the countryside, always makes good autumn colour, specialising in flaming mixtures of yellow and vermilion. The nineteenth-century squire who planted the woods in the immediate neighbourhood of my house obviously appreciated these effects, since he included plenty of Norway Maples in his plantings. Perhaps he also had in mind their spring colour, for the Norway Maple is unusual in that it flowers very early in the year, before coming into leaf, and the pale yellow blossom, adorning bare boughs in early April, can be very attractive.

The Sycamore, although not a native, has been here so long (it was probably introduced by the Romans) that it is entirely naturalised and has

FIELD MAPLE

ACER CAMPESTRE

Fig. 1

Winter twig of Field Maple. The tree is easily recognised in a mixed hedgerow or at the edge of a wood by the distinctive pale reddish-brown colour of its young shoots; these, and the small buds arising from them, are always set in opposite pairs, each pair at right angles to its neighbours.

Fig. 2

Twig with swelling buds on 26th May. The buds increase their size considerably before the leaves burst forth, and at this stage are often very colourful – a mixture of bright reds and yellows.

Fig. 3

The flowers are borne in erect corymbs, and here we see male flowers with fully developed stamens and female flowers with winged ovaries, in the same cluster. Young leaves are sometimes tinged, particularly around their margins, with red.

Fig. 4

By 6th August, the leaves have become dark green while their stalks are frequently pink or red. They are fairly small and have rounded lobes with sinuate margins and a few blunt teeth. The fruits consist of paired wings, generally set in a horizontal line, but sometimes at a shallow angle, or reflexed. They are often flushed with crimson.

Fig. 5

Autumn colour can be very striking, particularly where the Maple forms part of an old hedge: generally yellows and oranges, but in exceptional years deepening to scarlet, crimson and purple.

Fig. 2

Fig. 3

Fig. 1

Fig. 5

Fig. 4

SYCAMORE
I

ACER PSEUDOPLATANUS

Fig. 1

Winter twig of Sycamore; it is pale brown and bears green buds with brown-edged bud scales in opposite pairs.

Fig. 2

Swelling buds on 24th April. This specimen was taken from a young sapling, which accounts for the large size and good colour of the buds.

Fig. 3

Buds opening to reveal young leaves and flowers emerging together on 28th April.

Fig. 4

Leaves expanding on 4th May.

Sycamore (*Acer pseudoplatanus*).

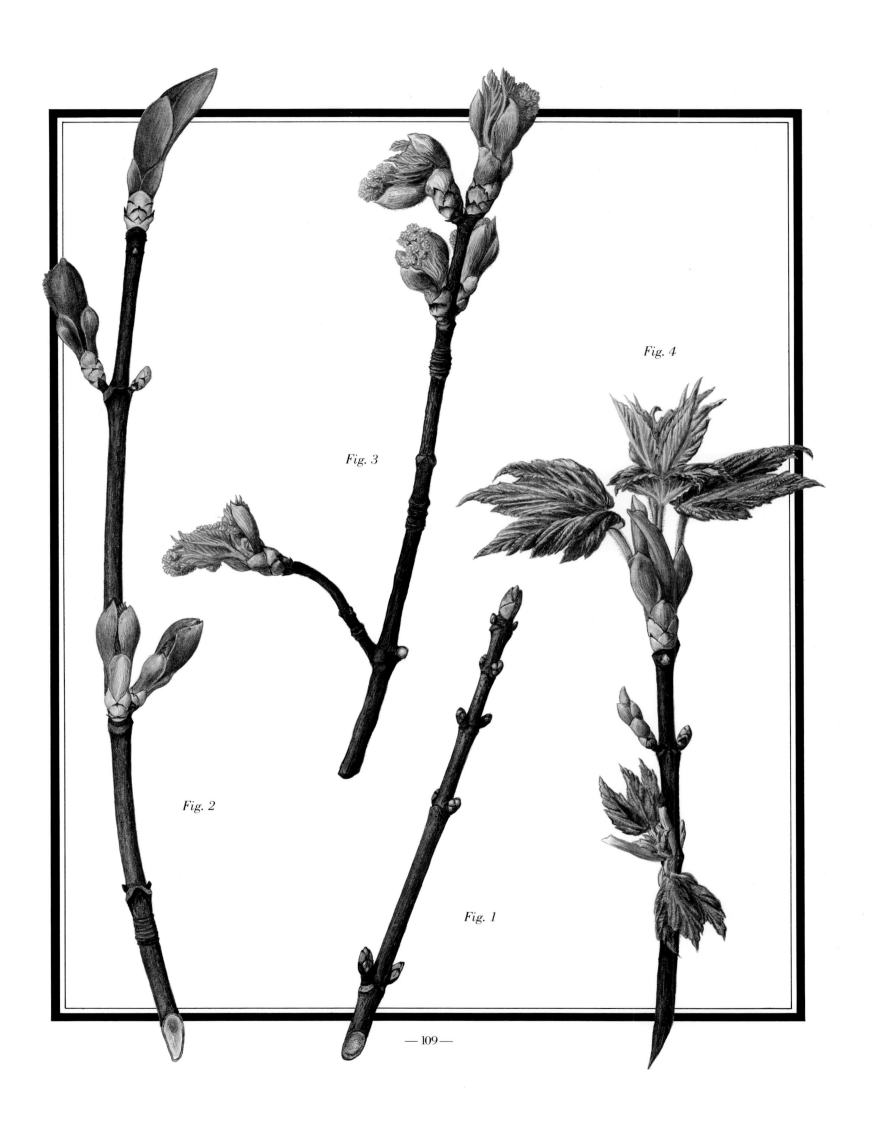

Fig. 4

Fig. 3

Fig. 2

Fig. 1

II

Fig.1

Young leaves and flowers of Sycamore on 22nd May. The racemes of flowers hang down, and male, female and sterile flowers can all be found on the same tree. The raceme on the left shows several female flowers with lobed ovaries and curling, two-cleft styles, among many sterile flowers with rudimentary pistils and stamens; that on the right has predominantly male flowers with fully developed stamens.

Fig.2

Leaves and fruit on 8th August. The leaves, borne in pairs, are now blackish-green above, grey-green below. They have five coarsely toothed lobes, of which the two basal ones, as with our other two Maples, are small. Leaf stalks are often tinged with red. The fruits consist of winged seeds, generally in pairs (sometimes three) set at an obtuse angle to each other, and hang down in dense clusters. The wings may be green or flushed, to a greater or lesser extent, with scarlet or crimson.

Fig.3

Sycamore is not famed for its autumn colour. Often the leaves are still a dingy green when they fall. I once drove through a grove of large Sycamores in Hampshire, which had all turned a good yellow (I had to get out of the car to assure myself that they *were* Sycamore), but this is uncommon. Where there is any colour, the mixture of green, yellow and brown illustrated here is typical. Young trees in woodland make the best show, with lovely, clear, creamy yellows gradually deepening to chrome-yellow and orange.

The Sycamore

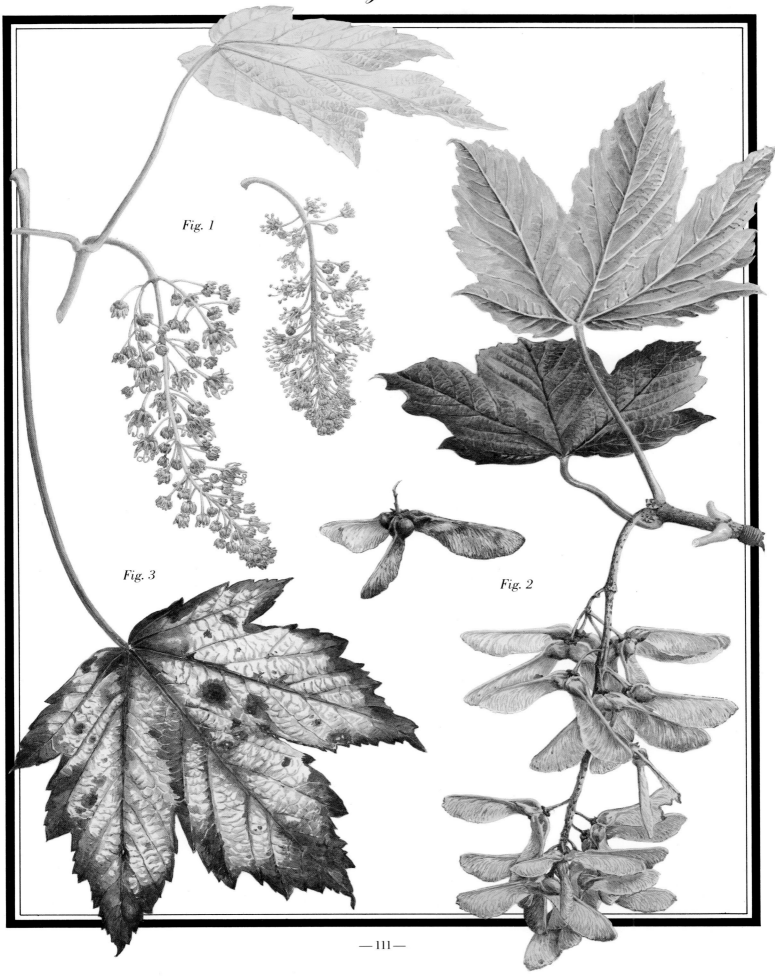

Fig. 1

Fig. 3

Fig. 2

NORWAY MAPLE

I

ACER PLATANOIDES

Fig. 1

Winter twig of Norway Maple: shiny, dark brown with plump crimson-brown buds in opposite pairs. This example, drawn at the end of February, has fruit stalks still attached.

Fig. 2

Buds swelling on 12th April. They become very large, displaying scales coated with black hairs.

Fig. 3

Flowering twig a few days later. The Norway Maple is the only one of our Maples to flower early, before coming into leaf. The handsome greenish-yellow flowers (the overall effect is bright yellow) make a fine show, often before the end of March. As with other Maples, flowers of both sexes can be found on the same tree. On this specimen, most of the flowers are male, but there is a female flower at the bottom right-hand edge of the lower cluster. Young leaves can be seen starting to emerge from the same buds.

Pair of Goldcrests (*Regulus regulus*). Goldcrests nest mainly in coniferous woodland, but are common in mixed woodland outside the breeding season.

Fig. 2

Fig. 1

Fig. 3

II

Fig.1

The leaves of Norway Maple are similar to those of Sycamore, but there are fewer teeth, while the sides of the lobes are almost parallel and their tips produced into long, narrow points. The fruits have wings that form a sharper angle than those of Field Maple, but less acute than those of Sycamore.

Fig.2

Fruits have turned brown and many will have fallen by early September.

Fig.3

Norway Maple colours early in the autumn – this leaf was drawn on 4th October – and can make a spectacular show, with bright orange and flaming reds predominating.

Norway Maple (*Acer platanoides*).

Fig. 1

Fig. 2

Fig. 3

spread to virtually every corner of these isles, a familiar constituent of almost any country scene, with the exception of heathland or high mountain terrain.

Some of the finest Sycamores are to be found in the Scottish border counties. I particularly remember admiring some splendid specimens growing in the park of Floors Castle on the River Tweed; but a rather more eccentric memory is of Sycamores growing in a part of the country not normally associated with trees of any kind.

The flat siltlands of the Holland district of Lincolnshire, bordering upon the Wash, are not to everyone's taste. Huge fields, divided by impeccably straight drainage dykes, stretch away to dim, featureless horizons. Dotted across the landscape are red-brick cottages or farm buildings, straw stacks, glasshouses, red-painted gates, perhaps the stump of an old windmill or the remains of a superseded sea wall. A row of wind-blown Poplars may mark the line of a road, and there will be tractors crawling ant-like hither and thither.

Over all arches the sky, immense and pervasive, an entity (unlike the city dweller's patch of blue or grey) that holds portents, impinges on every aspect of daily life, and cannot be ignored. The sea, too, from which most of that rich farmland has, over the centuries, been reclaimed, is a presence felt by the local people to be close even though perhaps seldom seen. For in that perfectly flat land you never catch a glimpse of the marshes, let alone the sea, until you have climbed to the top of a sea wall, and even then, if the tide is

Field Maple (*Acer campestre*).

out, the sea itself may be barely visible on the horizon. The sea walls form a boundary between the farmland, all order and economy, every field cultivated to the very edge of the dividing dykes, and the untamed wilderness of the marshes. Over the centuries, however, the frontiers of man's dominion have been pushed forward by successive reclamation schemes, and the wilderness has retreated until its suzerainty extends only over a narrow strip, the merest vestige of its former wide domain. These are the saltings, covered only by the high spring tides, and beyond them lie mile on mile of tidal mudflats.

I used to know some of the Wash marshes very well. They do not have a friendly aura, yet they possess the attraction of all wild places, with their own stark, elemental beauty governed by the seasons, the tides, the ever-changing skies, and enhanced by the haunting cries of the marsh birds – Curlew and Redshank, Herring Gull and Oystercatcher – and above all by the clamouring skeins of grey Geese that fly across the marshes at dawn and dusk in winter.

In such an environment it is a comfort to have a visible link with a more familiar, workaday world, and this was provided by the sea wall from which, on the marsh that I knew best, grew a line of Sycamores. The Sycamore is said to be one of the few deciduous trees able to withstand the perpetual onslaught of salt-laden winds, although I remember that there were also some healthy-looking Black Poplars on that wall. All the trees had a somewhat haggard look, resulting from their constant battle with the gales sweeping in from the North Sea. Yet they were robust enough, as if that long struggle had given them added strength, and I noticed, when I first walked along the sea wall in summer, that they carried heavy crowns of foliage.

THE LIMES

The Large-leaved Lime is found as a wild tree only in the Severn and Wye valleys, and in the West Riding of Yorkshire. I must sadly admit that I have not seen it growing in any of those locations, and know it only from a few planted trees in my own neighbourhood, one in woodland near my house and a few more in a Lime avenue not far away.

Our other native Lime, the Small-leaved, is found as a wild tree in scattered localities all over England and Wales, including a number of

COMMON LIME

I

TILIA X EUROPAEA

Fig.1

Twig of Common Lime in midwinter. The chestnut-brown buds are ovoid, bluntly pointed, and display two, or at most three, bud scales. They are set alternately on the twig.

Fig.2

Twig on 7th April with the buds just starting to swell. The twigs are brown, with the previous year's shoots olive-green.

Fig.3

Buds bursting a few days later. This twig is from a red-twigged cultivar, but twigs from ordinary trees are frequently tinged with crimson.

Fig.4

Young leaves on 8th May.

Common Lime (*Tilia* x *europaea*).

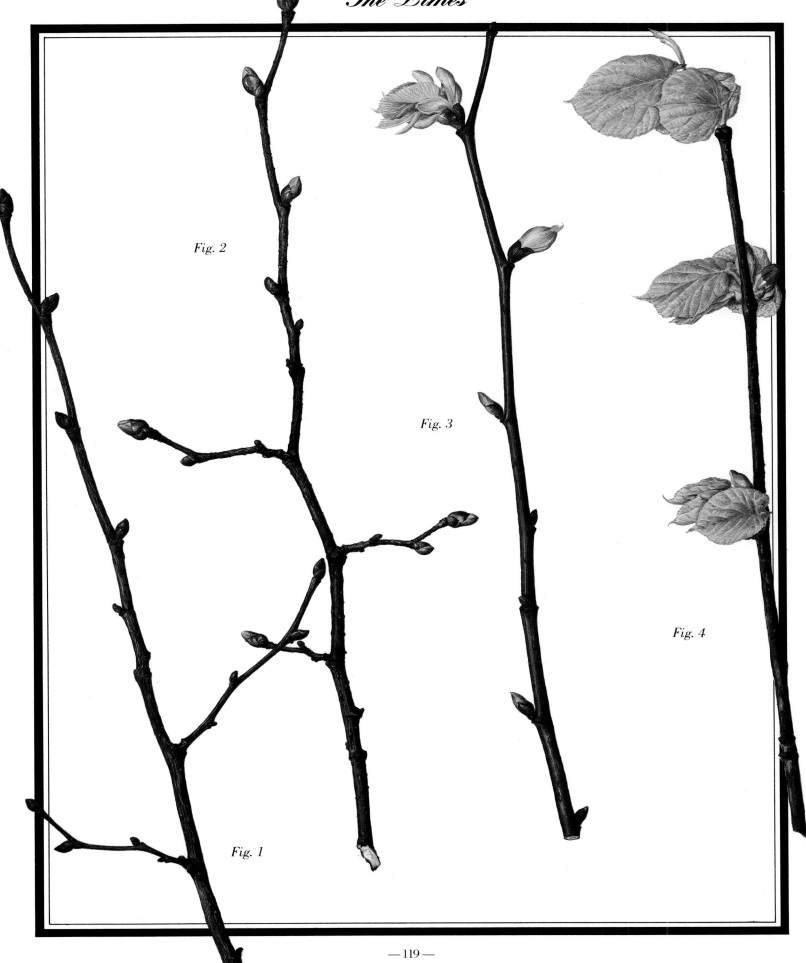

Fig. 2

Fig. 3

Fig. 4

Fig. 1

II

Fig. 1

Flowering twig of Common Lime on 12th July, showing the undersides of the leaves which are large, toothed and heart-shaped. They are glabrous, apart from little buff-coloured tufts of hairs in the axils of the veins on the undersides. The long petioles, however, and the shoots from which they spring, are clothed with short hairs. The sweet-scented flowers, beloved of bees, hang down in clusters on long stalks to which are attached long, narrow, pale green bracts. The flowers consist of five greenish-white sepals, alternating with as many very pale yellow petals. The stamens, with bright yellow anthers, are numerous and surround a pale green, pubescent ovary, from which rises a tall, slender style topped by a yellow, divided stigma.

Fig. 2

By 12th August, the leaves have become a darker green, and are likely to be sticky from the honeydew secreted by aphids. The fruits have ripened and are globular, grey-green and hairy.

Fig. 3

Fruits may be obovoid rather than spherical and show faint ribbing. In late summer, they start to fall, the bracts become brown and the fruits themselves shrivel.

Fig. 4

Limes are not renowned for their autumn colour. The leaves may fall a faded green, or may turn yellowish before fading to pale brown.

Lime Hawk Moth (*Mimas tiliae*).

Fig. 1

Fig. 4

Fig. 2

Fig. 3

SMALL-LEAVED
—AND—
LARGE-LEAVED
LIME

TILIA CORDATA AND TILIA PLATYPHYLLOS

Fig. 1

Winter twig of Small-leaved Lime. The twig is not noticeably different from that of other Limes, but the tree can be readily recognised from below by the fineness of its tracery. The twig is glabrous, either reddish or pale olive-brown; the buds may be green, brown or more or less crimson-tinged.

Fig. 2

Leaves and fruit of Small-leaved lime on 19th September. The leaves are small, shiny green above and glaucous below, with tufts of red-brown hairs in the vein axils on the underside, but otherwise glabrous. The fruits are markedly smaller than those of other Limes, globular, finely pubescent and without apparent ribs.

Fig. 3

Winter twig of Large-leaved Lime. Considerably stouter than that of *T. cordata*, with larger buds and, in my experience, both twig and buds showing more crimson colouring. It is pubescent, especially during spring and summer, and hard to distinguish from the twig of *T. europaea*.

Fig. 4

Leaves and fruit of Large-leaved Lime in early October. The leaves are large, but not necessarily much larger than those of Common Lime. A surer distinction is that they are pubescent above and on the veins beneath. The fruit fall is densely pubescent and prominently ribbed. Nail galls, seen on the green leaf, are also common on the leaves of *T. europaea*.

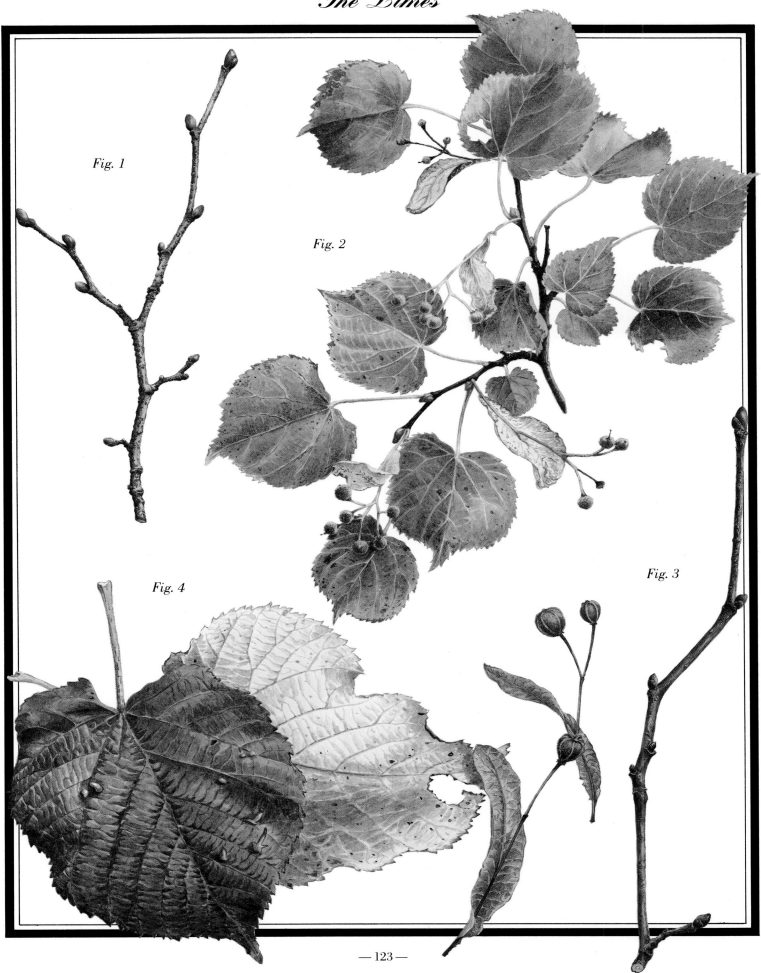

Fig. 1

Fig. 2

Fig. 3

Fig. 4

woodland areas in north-central Essex, where it is thought to be indigenous and where it regenerates from seed. One of those is Chalkney Wood in the parish of Earls Colne, but my specimens for the colour plates were taken from one of the huge old trees that make up the Lime Avenue (predominantly Common Lime) at Coldham Hall in Suffolk.

The Common Lime is a natural hybrid between the two foregoing species, and although I know it from many different situations, including the parks and avenues of numerous country houses and at least one local wood, for me it is always *the* deciduous tree of churchyards, just as Yew is the typical conifer.

I have a predilection for churchyards which is far from being morbid. Despite their primary function, churchyards can be places of abundant life, so long as members of the local community do not get too enthusiastic with the clippers and the mowing machine. Churchyard swards, if not cut too frequently or too close, can become rich in wild flowers; tombstones and the church walls and buttresses attract ferns, mosses, liverworts and lichens; bushes and trees provide nesting sites for birds, and the whole churchyard area, if managed sensitively, can become an interesting and lovely little nature reserve. I have seen churchyards where large areas of old tombstones have been cleared to make way for the motor mower, and this simultaneous destruction of local history and wildlife habitat is to my mind nothing short of vandalism.

Fortunately, most country churchyards are still pleasant places in which to while away the odd hour, and the great Lime trees casting their shadows impartially among the intimations of mortality and symbols of immortality contribute largely to the atmosphere of peace and tranquillity. They are at their best just after midsummer when the fragrant yellow flowers hang down under their canopies of soft, pale green leaves, and Bees, feasting on the nectar, fill the air with their soporific drone.

THE ASH

On the lawn in front of my cousin's house in Wiltshire stood a large Ash tree, with a swing hanging from one of its lower boughs. It was probably the tree from which I learnt to recognise the species; certainly it was the first Ash that I knew as an individual. In fact, it was as a young boy, while staying with my cousin, that I first came to identify many of the common British trees. His father, a skilled amateur craftsman, had made a turntable for the breakfast table consisting of wedge-shaped segments, each of a different wood and including a sample from every species of tree that grew on the estate. The names of the various timbers were written underneath and excited my curiosity to the extent that I gradually succeeded in matching many of them with the trees from which they came. One of the first must have been the very pale segment that came from the Ash tree on the lawn.

The house stood among some small hills, or rather undulations, beneath the escarpment of Salisbury Plain. Up on the chalk downland, Beech was the predominant tree, and on the loams of the Vale of Avon, Elm, but on the greensand in between there was a wide variety, including a lot of Ash. At the beginning of each holiday, I would make for a nearby area of Ash coppice, where there was a large Badger set, and cut a stick for my long walks across the plain, or among the woods and small Elm-girdled meadows in the vale in the company of Rufus, the Cocker Spaniel. I have always had the habit of taking a stick on walks and, like a penknife in the pocket, I never understand how other people manage without one.

The Ash is another of those ubiquitous trees that one can expect to find in almost any part of the country. When I first came to live in Essex, I soon got to know one old Ash. Trees, like people, gain character with age, at least visually. This old tree was partly hollow, and as it stood on the steep slope of a little meadow that formed a narrow valley, its roots on the lower side were to some extent exposed, serving as flying buttresses. In the sandy soil beneath the tree, rabbits had dug their burrows among the roots. One day in early summer, the ewes and their lambs, which had been put onto the meadow for a few days to graze it off, were moved to some other place, about a quarter of a mile away. Ten days later, as I was walking down the valley meadow, I heard, to my surprise, the feeble but unmistakable bleat of a lamb; yet no lamb was

ASH

I

FRAXINUS EXCELSIOR

Fig. 1

The typical colour of Ash twigs is a pale, faintly greenish, grey. This, combined with the sooty black buds in opposite pairs, makes the Ash instantly recognisable, even in winter.

Fig. 2

Twig, bearing a dense cluster of mainly male flowers, on 30th April. The Ash comes into flower long before the leaves appear, and although some trees bear predominantly male flowers, and others predominantly female, flowers of both sexes, as well as hermaphrodite flowers, can all occur on the same tree.

Fig. 3

This twig, also drawn on 30th April, bears mainly female flowers, which tend to be produced on longer stalks. Like the male flowers, the female flowers are very simple, consisting of a pistil with an extended style and cleft stigma.

Fig. 4

Ashes come late into leaf (always long after Oak despite the old saying, 'Ash before Oak, there will be a soak') and here the young leaves are barely showing on 15th May. At the base of this twig can be seen several female flowers due to develop into fruit, and a withered clump of male flowers on the right.

Fig. 5

The next stage, a week or so later, with young leaves emerged and immature fruits.

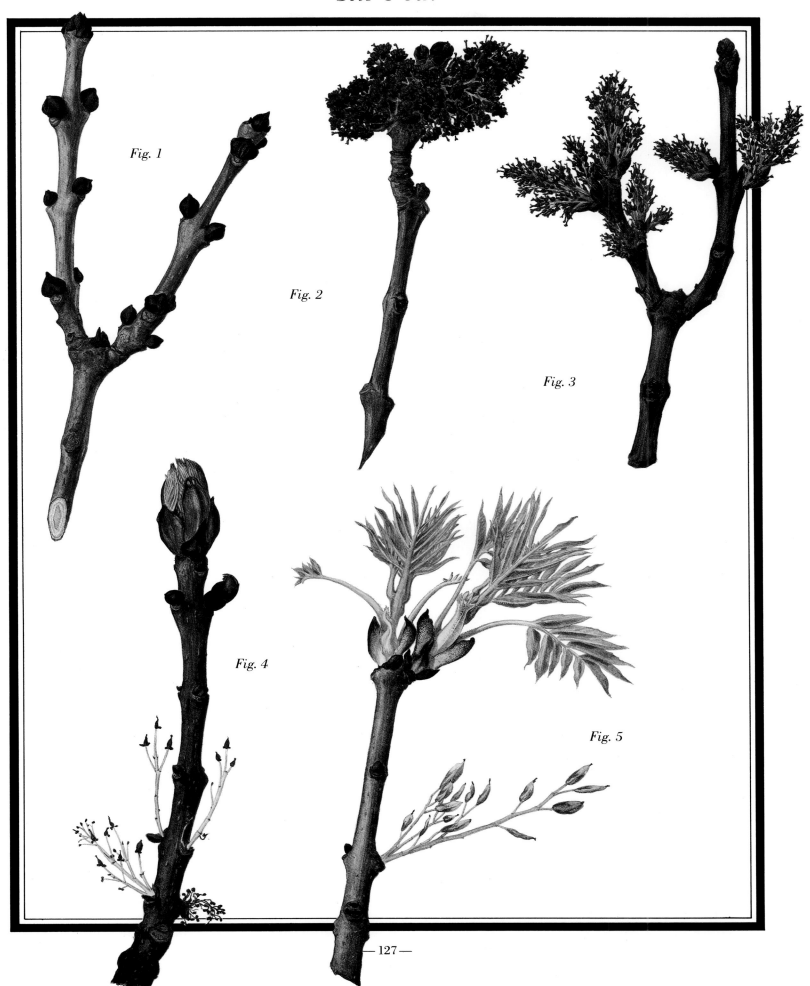

Fig. 1

Fig. 2

Fig. 3

Fig. 4

Fig. 5

II

Fig. 1

Leafy twig of Ash on 1st July. Leaves are borne in opposite pairs – though this is not clear from the drawing – and are pinnate with (usually) five opposite pairs of finely toothed, lanceolate leaflets and a single leaflet at the apex. What appears to be a stalk with leaves on either side is, in fact, the midrib of a single compound leaf. This twig also bears a cluster of 'keys', the name generally given to the fruits of Ash.

Fig. 2

Ash 'keys' on 7th October, now turned brown, but still on the tree, where some may persist through the whole of the following winter.

Fig. 3

The majority of Ash leaves fall while still green. If they acquire any colour, it is an insipid shade of yellow.

Ash (*Fraxinus excelsior*).

Fig. 3

Fig. 1

Fig. 2

in sight, nor should there have been. After much puzzled searching, I realised that the sound came from *underneath* the Ash tree. To cut a long story short, I had to fetch help, with rabbiting grafts and a chain saw to cut through one of the big roots, before we could extract the lamb, which had fallen into a cavity deep beneath the tree. With some misgivings, we took it, a poor, skinny little thing, but still able to totter, down to the field where the sheep were then grazing. To our surprise, after such a long period, its bleats were almost immediately answered by its mother, a large old ewe whose lack of complaint at the loss of a lamb was explained by the fact that she was still feeding its twin. The lost lamb had a good, long suck, and in time recovered completely from its ordeal.

THE LONDON PLANE

*I*t could be argued that there is little justification for including the London Plane in a book purporting to deal only with trees one is liable to meet with in the course of a country walk, and I must admit that none of the rural specimens I know grow beyond the confines of a garden fence. I feel, however, that the tree occupies such a special place in English minds and hearts, albeit mainly from its use in cities, that it deserves to be made the exception to the rule.

The London Plane is a hybrid between the Oriental Plane *(Platanus orientalis)* and the American Plane *(P. occidentalis)*, and arose — no one is certain where — about the middle of the seventeenth century. Trees planted in England around 1680 are still flourishing, so it may well prove to be a tree of unusual longevity.

The group of trees of which I have the fondest memories (and I used one of them for the 'winter tree' drawing) was certainly over two hundred years old, probably coeval with the creation of the artificial lake by which they stood, and all part of a grand scheme by which gardens were laid out to complement major extensions made during the reign of Queen Anne to a William and Mary manor house. They were trees of exceptional grace and beauty at all times of the year: in winter, with their noble symmetry, dappled bark and long, pendulous, contorted shoots; in summer, with their great mass of light green foliage, and in autumn, with their fine colour. But I found them specially fascinating in early spring; when their long shoots carried, for

London Plane (*Platanus* x *acerifolia*).

a brief spell, velvet-soft golden leaves and female flowers in the form of bright crimson spheres. Daffodils, Narcissi and pink Cuckoo flowers grew all around them, and on the lake Mallard ducks led flotillas of downy young, or rested under the trailing shoots of Weeping Willows while the ducklings darted about in search of floating insects.

THE HORSE CHESTNUT

The Horse Chestnut is a robust, no-nonsense kind of tree, shaped in summer rather like a large tea-cosy, especially when it grows in parkland and has its lower branches and foliage browsed off to an even height. I consider it more attractive in winter when its stout brown branches and twigs make bold, swirling patterns and the huge buds show up clearly.

Particularly handsome then are old garden trees which have never been browsed, and whose lower branches sweep down to the ground before curling upwards again at their extremities.

LONDON PLANE

I

PLATANUS X ACERIFOLIA

Fig. 1

Plane tree twigs are stout, generally green on the underside, reddish-brown above and often speckled with white. The buds are conical, set in a rather haphazard spiral, each one enclosed by a single red-brown bud-scale, and almost encircled by the leaf scar since in summer, the bud is concealed by the swollen base of the leaf stalk.

Fig. 2

Buds swelling and breaking open on 29th April.

Fig. 3

Flowering twig on 15th May. At this stage, the young leaves are very beautiful, thickly pubescent and velvety to the touch, golden-green above, silver-green below. Male and female flowers are borne on separate catkins, both in the form of round 'bobbles'. The small, yellowish-green bobbles are the male flowers, while the catkin near the apex of the twig bears female flowers, which appear larger by reason of the crowded crimson styles that arise from them.

Fig. 4

Fruits ripening on 3rd October. These are particularly fine specimens taken from a tree in Regent's Park Zoo.

Fig. 2

Fig. 4

Fig. 1

Fig. 3

Fig. 1

Leaves of London Plane show considerable variation, but are generally similar in shape to those of the *Acer* species, although always distinguishable by the hollow bases of the leaf stalks. They also tend to be larger, the largest I found being 12″ from base to apex and 16″ in width. They are leathery in texture, and glabrous, and remain a bright shade of green through the summer.

Fig. 2

Leaf displaying typical autumn colour on 8th November. Fruits, which vary considerably in size, have by now developed into a mass of small, hard nuts and are turning brown.

Fig. 3

Fruits often stay on the tree through the winter. These had fallen from the tree in May, and are starting to break up, releasing the individual seeds, each of which has a tuft of buff-coloured hairs to aid its dispersal on the wind. The shredded stalk is typical.

Fig. 1

Fig. 2

Fig. 3

HORSE CHESTNUT

I

AESCULUS HIPPOCASTANUM

Fig. 1

The winter twig of Horse Chestnut is very stout, pale brown or reddish, and dotted with small 'lenticels' or breathing pores. The buds are the familiar 'sticky buds', large and shiny brown, and are borne in opposite pairs, with a branching pair of buds or a single very big bud at the apex of the twig. Below each bud is a large leaf scar resembling the print of a horse's hoof.

Fig. 2

Bud starting to open on 19th April. This twig was taken from a young tree struggling to grow on rather poor soil, which accounts for the crowded leaf scars immediately below the bud.

Fig. 3

Young leaves emerging about the same time. At this stage, they are thickly covered by a mesh of sticky, fawn filaments which will disappear as the leaves expand.

Fig. 4

Young leaves growing fast and leaflets separating on 24th April.

Fig. 1

Fig. 2

Fig. 3

Fig. 4

II

Fig.1

Inflorescence of Horse Chestnut on 19th May. The individual flowers are white, with frilly-edged petals and long stamens with white filaments tipped by orange anthers. The central area of the corolla starts off lemon-yellow and progresses through orange to pink and crimson. Since flowers at all stages are present at the same time, the result is very colourful.

Fig.2

The compound, palmate leaf has from three to seven leaflets, and is very large, frequently more than 15″ across. In midsummer, it is dark green.

Horse Chestnut
(*Aesculus hippocastanum*).

Fig. 2

Fig. 1

III

Fig.1

Horse Chestnut fruits and autumn leaves in October. Leaves on some trees turn very early, and the colour can be extremely fine, with bright yellows, coppery-browns, reds and crimsons. The fruit is globular, pale green and covered, to a greater or lesser extent, with sharp, though fairly soft, spines. Towards the end of September, the husks start to split, exposing either one or two seeds – the familiar glossy brown 'conkers' – which fall from the tree throughout October.

Fig.2

Fruit husks and seeds in October.

Fig. 1

Fig. 2

Although its overall shape may lack elegance, its various parts make up for this, with something to offer in every season of the year.

First of all, there are the familiar sticky buds, so satisfyingly large and glistening, which are at their best as spring approaches and the warmer days cause their resin coating to liquefy. I always like to bring some small branches into the house, put them in water, and watch the buds voluptuously swelling and unfolding, and the young leaves and incipient flower clusters breaking out and expanding against the mesh of gossamer threads that binds them.

In May the trees become decked from top to bottom with a mass of white candle-flame flower panicles, and Bumblebees gather from all around to join in Bacchanalian revelries while the nectar lasts.

Later in the year, there are the fine and varied autumn colours of the leaves and, best of all, the conkers. Finding, examining and handling the first conkers of the year are among those pleasures that never pall. No matter that many summers may have passed since you last got busy with skewer and knotted string and set out to challenge the current champion, the feeling that you get as you open the spiky capsules and reveal those glossy, delicately grained nuts lying in their white, silken beds, remains the same. As you open the caskets, there is the merest scintilla of a sweet, fruity scent, then the nuts slide, so smooth and pristine, into your hand, and who can resist kneading them between the fingers and rubbing them against the face to heighten the polish?

Just as Lime trees remind me of churchyards, Horse Chestnuts, with less reason perhaps, remind me of village cricket matches. Partly, I think because the cricket pitch in a local village, which I often pass, is bordered by Horse Chestnuts – although of the red-flowered variety, *Aesculus* x *carnea* – but certainly also on account of a match in which I played many years ago, when I was at Oxford, against a Cotswold village team. I was playing in a college club side which specialised in village cricket, membership of which was much sought after because the matches always involved a lengthy and excellent lunch, and ended with a convivial evening drinking with the opposing side at some local pub. I remember this particular match because the day, the setting and the lunch (which included Lobster salad) were all so perfect. On one side of the ground was a lovely old house of mellow Cotswold stone, surrounded by gardens full of old-fashioned roses and herbaceous borders, and on the other by a delectable chalk stream. Opposite the house, on the far side of the ground, stood a Beech hanger, and dotted all around the perimeter of the ground, ready to receive the sixes in their dark, leafy crowns, were Horse Chestnuts. I can still remember some of the events of that game, including a terrible slogger among the opposition (could he have been the village blacksmith?) and the ball which bowled me out for an inglorious score of three; but chiefly I remember sitting under the shade of the Horse Chestnuts while waiting to bat, enjoying the balmy day and the feeling of drowsy repletion, listening to the click of bat on ball, the occasional cries of the fielders and ripples of applause from the spectators, and thinking what a very delightful way this was to spend a summer afternoon.

THE SORBUS SPECIES

I was hunting through a wood near my house one October day a few years back, looking for fungi, and had come to an area where three good edible species – Shaggy Parasols, Wood Mushrooms and Wood Blewits – were all growing in abundance, when some leaves among the many scattered on the ground around me caught my attention. They varied in colour from yellow and deep red to shiny tobacco brown, and bore a superficial resemblance to Maple leaves, being similarly lobed although larger and narrower. I recognised them as the leaves of that least known of all our native trees, the Wild Service Tree, and I then spent a frustrating ten minutes trying to locate the tree from which they had fallen. Eventually I discovered it standing, as if loth to be recognised, between a Field Maple and a group of Elms. I stood immediately beneath it, and, peering up through its branches I could see that its crown, hardly visible from a distance, was a wonderful mixture of fiery orange and bright chestnut tints. The Wild Service Tree is such a shy species that it is small wonder few people recognise it or even know it exists. Nearly always it is a single specimen, and frequently it is buried deep in the heart of old mixed deciduous woodland. Whenever I have found one, it has been by noticing first the fallen leaves, as was the case with one growing even nearer to my house, barely fifty yards away, in fact, on the other side of the cart track. Again, its neighbour on one side was a Field Maple, on the other a Sycamore, and I had walked past it every day of the summer without realising its identity. In the spring its corymbs of small white flowers are not very conspicuous, while its fruits consist of rather sparse olive-green berries (more accurately pomes) which later turn a dull brown. There is something mysterious and intriguing about this tree, so self-effacing and so solitary, that has yet survived from prehistoric times. Folklore ascribes it various magical properties, and its fruits, sometimes known as 'chequers', have formed part of the herbalist's pharmacopoeia at least since the Roman era.

If the tree is difficult to recognise in the summer, it is all the more so in winter, having no special characteristics of shape or habit; and its buds are so similar to those of Hazel as to be barely distinguishable except that they are set spirally, while the Hazel's are alternate.

Rowan (*Sorbus aucuparia*).

The tree near my house stands at the corner of a small meadow where Cowslips and Cuckoo-flowers grow in profusion in the spring and where, in summer, two house cows and their calves graze, standing knee-deep among Buttercups and Oxeye Daisies. In the autumn the leaves of the Wild Service Tree fall on the meadow and on the muddy cart track, or float on the surface of a black, tree-girt pond nearby. At the foot of the tree, great mounds of Bramble overhang a deep ditch. This is a tiny remnant of an ancient landscape, unchanged over many generations, and it is in such habitats that the Wild Service Tree must be sought.

The cart track beside which the Wild Service Tree stands continues, straight as a die, between wide fields of wheat and barley until it meets the road, some quarter of a mile distant. There, on the right, stands a fine specimen of a closely related species, the Whitebeam; but this is a planted tree, not native in East Anglia as it is in the west country and elsewhere on chalk and limestone soils. It is much more easily recognised than the Wild Service: of moderate size, with upswept branches and a broad, rounded crown, in summer its large leaves with their white-felted undersides, make it unmistakeable.

The Whitebeam belongs to a species whose varieties and hybrids have been much disputed by botanists, and I chiefly remember it as a wild tree by one of its subspecies, the Rock Whitebeam (var. *rupicola*). I was spending a week botanising in the Derbyshire Dales, and encountered a group of small trees of this race among some carboniferous limestone rocks at the head of a deep valley above the River Wye. It was the first time I had come across any Whitebeams in the wild, and they were among a number of 'firsts' which made that a memorable day, including Bloody Geranium, Melancholy Thistle and Nottingham Catchfly; and, among the ferns, Wall Rue Spleenwort and Limestone Polypody.

The third of our *Sorbus* species, Rowan or Mountain Ash, is another tree seldom seen growing wild in this part of the country, although frequently planted in gardens. I can think of one or two rather sorry specimens in local woodlands, presumably sprung from bird-sown seeds, but the tree does not thrive on our rich soils, and for me the name Rowan inevitably conjures up pictures of Scotland, and in particular of autumn days fishing for salmon on the River Brora in Sutherland. The lower river, below Loch Brora, plunges

ROWAN

SORBUS AUCUPARIA

Fig. 1

Rowan twig in winter, showing the very large buds which curve into a blunt point. They are purplish and clothed with long grey hairs.

Fig. 2

The numerous small, creamy-white flowers of Rowan on 6th June. They are borne in corymbs at the ends of short, leafy branches.

Fig. 3

Leaves and fruit on 12th September. The leaves are pinnately compound, very similar to those of Ash, although unrelated – hence the name Mountain Ash often given to this species. The berries, beloved of birds, hang in dense clusters and progress from yellow through orange to bright scarlet by mid-August. Inside, they are bright yellow.

Fig. 4

The typical autumn colour. Rowan leaves colour early and trees are often bare before the end of October.

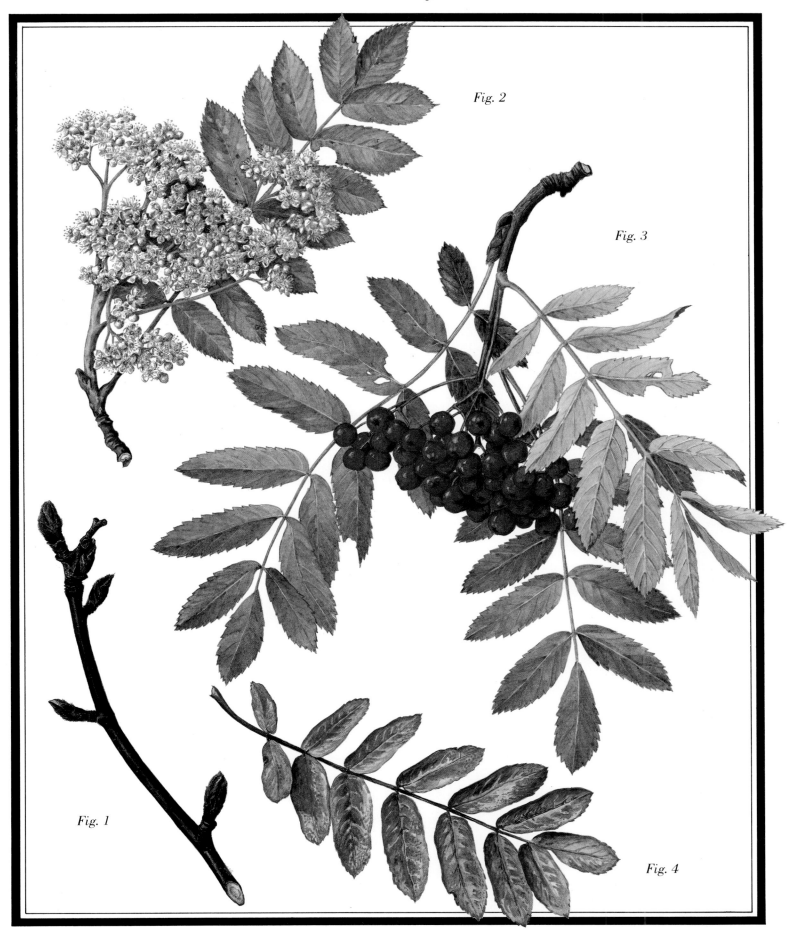

Fig. 1

Fig. 2

Fig. 3

Fig. 4

WHITEBEAM

SORBUS ARIA

Fig.1

Winter twigs of Whitebeam are stout, with large, pointed, hairy, green buds. They may be brown or green, and when young are covered with patches of white pubescence.

Fig.2

Young leaves and flowers emerging together on 26th April. At this stage they are very similar to those of Wild Service Tree, but the bud-scales of Whitebeam do not become so elongated.

Fig.3

Flowering twig on 28th May. The white flowers are similar to those of *S. aucuparia*, but generally less numerous. The leaves are large, oval, with finely toothed edges, green and glabrous on the upper side, felted with white down beneath.

Fig.4

Leaves and ripe fruit on 21st October. The fruits are berries, yellowish to bright red. Autumn leaf colour tends towards yellows and chestnut-browns.

Whitebeam (*Sorbus aria*).

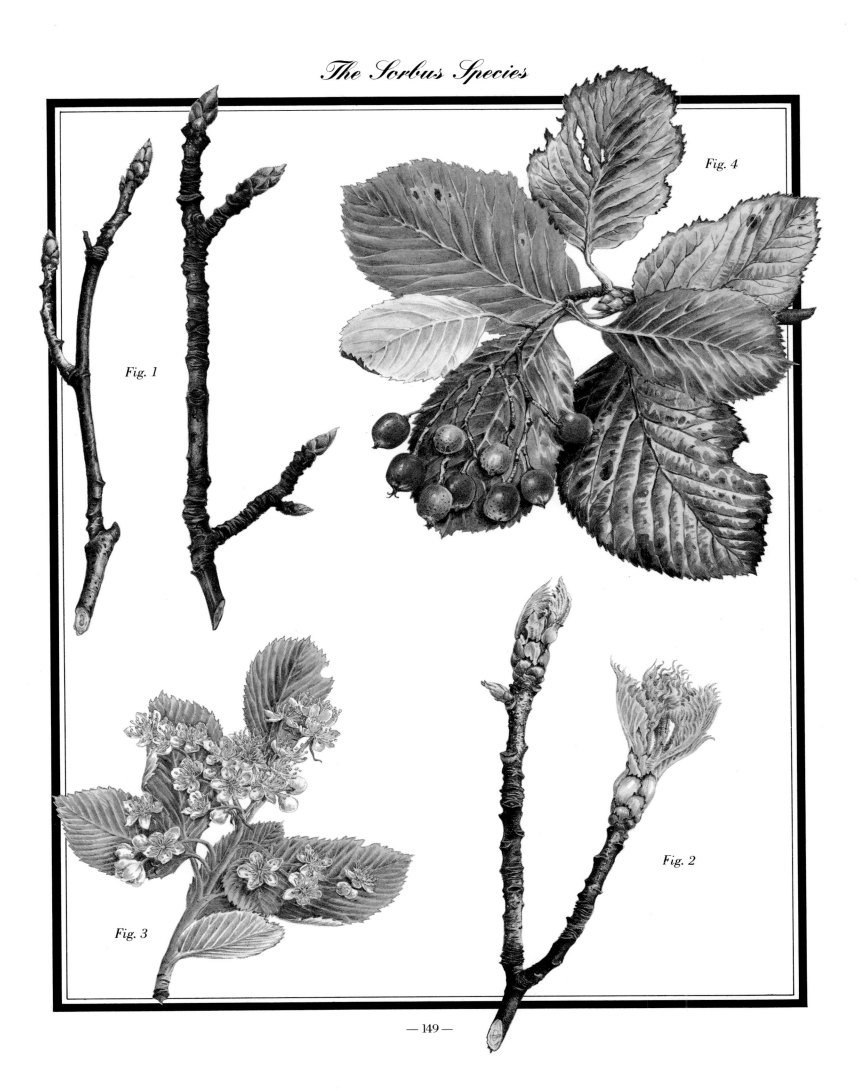

Fig. 4

Fig. 1

Fig. 3

Fig. 2

WILD SERVICE TREE

SORBUS TORMINALIS

Fig. 1

Winter twig of Wild Service Tree: reddish-brown, covered with small warts and patches of white pubescence. The buds are plump and shiny green with ragged brown margins to the bud scales. They are very similar to the buds of Hazel, but are borne spirally instead of alternately.

Fig. 2

Bud-burst on 25th April. The young leaves are silvery-grey at this stage, and covered with downy hairs which soon disappear.

Fig. 3

Flowering twig on 6th June. The flowers are borne in a loose corymb, and have white petals, creamy-white anthers and a smell reminiscent of Hawthorn flowers.

Fig. 4

Leaves and fruit on 4th August. The leaves are often mistaken for those of Field Maple, but are more elongated, and their margins are very finely serrate. The fruit is an olive-green or brown berry, covered with small reddish pimples and a fine white pubescence.

Fig. 5

Leaves and fallen fruit on 7th November. The autumn colour is generally a splendid deep orange, in some years progressing to dark red, but more often becoming tobacco-brown before falling.

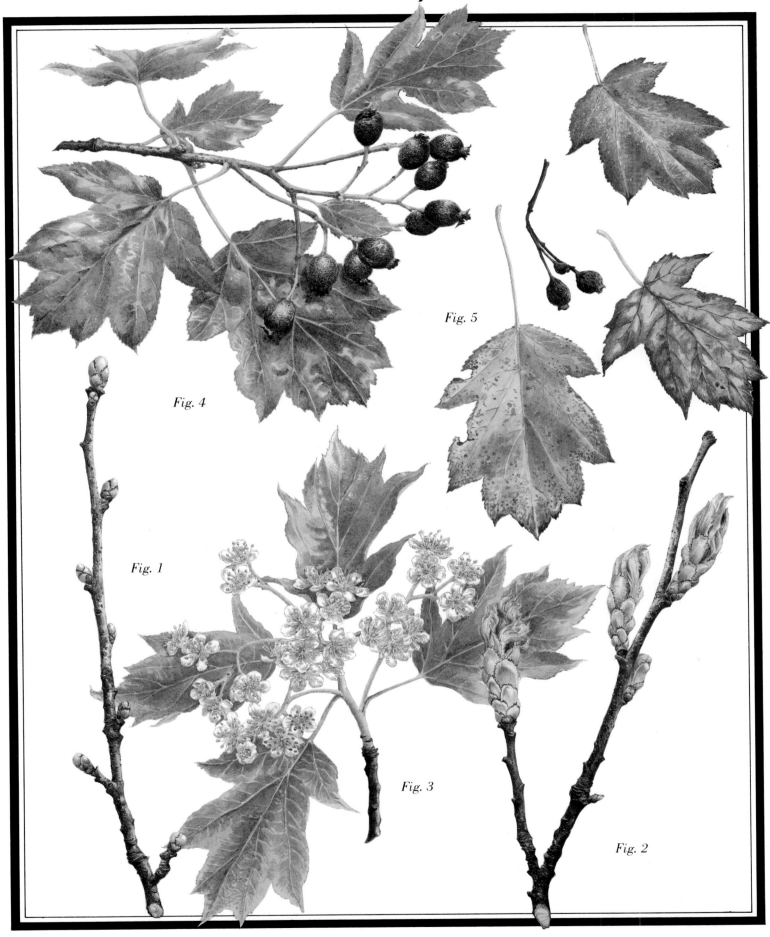

Fig. 5

Fig. 4

Fig. 1

Fig. 3

Fig. 2

down through a series of narrow gorges, interspersed by the most delectable pools, on its short journey to the sea. It passes through a countryside of low hills where rough pastures merge into slopes of russet Bracken dotted with Pines and Birches and grazing sheep. But is is the Rowans that stay in the mind: with their orange leaves and hanging clusters of scarlet fruit, they stand in droves around the cottage gardens and the crofters' farmsteads, they line the tracks that lead down to the river and fringe the dark woods, and their bright colours flame on the river's banks and are reflected in the deep water of the pools.

THE HAWTHORN

The Hawthorn is one of those native trees which naturalists like because it provides food, shelter or both for so many different creatures, from the birds nesting among its branches down to tiny insects living in the interstices of its bark. Recently I made rough lists, for each tree genus, of the larger moth species (Macrolepidoptera) for whom the tree was the sole or principal food plant. The Willows, in particular the Sallow, won hands down with well over a hundred species. The native Oaks and the Birches came joint second, each with about eighty-eight species, and the Hawthorn third with something over fifty species. Since most of the Hawthorn found in the country consists of hedge material, the importance to wildlife of conserving our few remaining hedges will be readily appreciated.

Given the chance, the Hawthorn will grow into a small but undeniable tree, with a single, sturdy bole and a compact crown. In my area, several farmers have let Hawthorns grow up into trees at intervals along some hedges, and this seems an extremely good idea since they perform the necessary functions of hedgerow trees (for instance, as singing perches for hedge-nesting birds, without which many species will not breed), and yet do not send out huge root systems to rob the soil of nutrients or cast an unacceptable amount of shade. Also, they do not suffer from the defect which Blackthorn exhibits as a hedging plant, of sending up suckers at a distance from the hedgerow.

I am glad to say that during my farming years I was responsible for planting a five-hundred-yard-long Hawthorn hedge, which I hope future owners of the land will cherish and maintain. All too often, one is more likely to see old hedges destroyed than new ones created. The economic arguments used to justify this state of affairs are very compelling; but it is a pity that there are not more landowners (fortunately there are a few) whose actions are not governed exclusively by such considerations.

I once had the opportunity to lay, under expert tutelage, several chains of overgrown hedgerow dividing two large Leicestershire pastures. Nowadays, every time I pass a hedge that has been mutilated by a mechanical flail, with branches cracked and shattered, or stripped of bark, with not even an attempt at clearing up the damage afterwards, I am reminded of that experience and the care and skill a good hedger was expected to put into every stroke of his axe or billhook. Even the 'heel' left when a Hawthorn layer had been lowered into place had to be removed by a difficult upward stroke of the billhook, ensuring that the cut surface matched exactly the cut surface on the layer, enabling rain water to run off, rather than being trapped in the cleft, absorbed into, and eventually rotting, the stool. This degree of careful craftsmanship is impossible on a widespread scale today, when manpower is scarce and barbed wire fences so much easier to erect and maintain, but that is no excuse for the barbarous treatment that many hedges receive when modern equipment, which works well enough when used to trim up young growth, is employed to batter large, old hedges into submission.

THE CRAB APPLE

When I first set out to find a Crab Apple from which to gather specimens to draw, I imagined that the task would be quite simple. It was autumn, when the trees should be bearing fruit, making them easier to locate (for they tend to hide themselves among other trees in ancient hedgerows and on the fringes of woods).

I started by noting down all the wild Apple trees that I could remember having seen in the locality over the years: two or three on roadsides where their squandered fruit would lie in drifts against the bank each autumn, one in a huge, overgrown hedge beside a bridleway I had often ridden in past winters, several in hedges around meadowland where cattle browsed the lower branches, another at the edge of some Oak woodland not far from my

HAWTHORN

CRATAEGUS MONOGYNA

Fig. 1

Winter twig. This example, with its small stalked buds and straight needle-sharp thorns, is taken from vigorous young hedgerow growth. Twigs from mature trees tend to be more knobbly and much less thorny.

Fig. 2

Twig in late May, showing young leaves and corymbs of white flowers with pink or crimson anthers. Trees whose flowers are tinged, to a greater or lesser extent, with pink, are fairly common.

Fig. 3

Leaves and fruit on 23rd September. The leaves are deeply divided into coarsely toothed lobes, shiny green above, grey-green below. The fruit is a scarlet berry which later darkens and becomes more crimson.

Fig. 4

A group of autumn leaves, showing the wide range of colour from pale yellow through to deep purple.

Hawthorn (*Crataegus monogyna*).

Fig. 2

Fig. 1

Fig. 3

Fig. 4

CRAB APPLE

MALUS SYLVESTRIS

Fig. 1

Winter twigs of Crab Apple are long, slender and whippy, and may form a tangled mass in the crowns of old trees. The buds are small, the bud scales purplish and fringed with white hairs. Spurs sometimes develop into thorns.

Fig. 2

Flower buds and young leaves on 30th April.

Fig. 3

Flowering twig on 15th May. The flowers are small compared with most domestic varieties of Apple, the petals white tinged with pink; margins of petals and anthers are hairy. Crab Apple flowers are fragrant, with a scent not unlike that of Honeysuckle.

Fig. 4

Leaves and fruit on 14th October. The leaves are rounded and evenly toothed. In autumn, they acquire brown and purplish tints. The apples are very small and bitter to the taste, green with white speckles, sometimes becoming flushed or speckled with red, finally turning golden-yellow with brown speckles. They are broader than they are long, with deep depressions at either end of the core and notably long stalks (an important feature in distinguishing the true Crab from wild-grown hybrids). Some apples may remain on the tree right through the winter.

Fig. 2

Fig. 3

Fig. 4

Fig. 1

Crab Apple (*Malus sylvestris*).

house. Altogether, I had nearly a dozen trees from which to choose, but when I started visiting each in turn, the task began to appear less straightforward. One tree was nearly dead from old age and the few remaining sappy branches bore leaves but no fruit. Two that had stood in a hedge between meadows had vanished, together with the hedge and even the meadows, the latter having been replaced by a bland expanse of wheat stubble, while all the others turned out to be descendants, perhaps planted, perhaps bird-sown, of orchard Codlins and Pippins. None bore the characteristics of the true Crab Apple.

Several weeks later, I had occasion to visit a neighbouring market town, and taking a favourite route more notable for its scenery than its convenience, I found myself at a spot where the River Colne crosses a narrow lane. An old weatherboarded mill, now converted to a dwelling house, stands there and on either side are water meadows and receding vistas of Poplar and Willow trees. Gnats danced in the mellow sunlight of an Indian summer, and from a nearby farm came the rich smell of pigs. As I peered through my car windscreen at the swift waters of the river, swelled by recent rain, wondering if I dare risk the crossing, it occurred to me that somewhere back up the lane, while my mind had been on other things, I had driven over some small, green apples on the road. Quickly I reversed the car, feeling that with regard to the ford discretion was probably, in any event, the better part of valour, and drove back up the hill.

There, sure enough, were the apples strewn about the road, and having parked my car in a gateway, I went to inspect them and found to my delight that they were veritable Crabs. The gateway opened onto a hilly meadow dotted with Hawthorn bushes and led down to a piece of boggy land where a herd of bullocks stood knee-deep in muddy water among tussocks of rushes. It was a spot pleasantly untouched by the hand of the agricultural improver. The old Apple tree grew beside the hanging post of the gate and the oak rails of a fence had been nailed to its side. It was gnarled, scarred and leaning, and though some of its lower branches had been lopped off, others carried a crown that was a dense and tangled mass of slender twigs among which gleamed a multitude of tiny green and yellow apples, some flushed with red. On the other side of the gate stood an equally venerable Hawthorn. The two trees leaned towards each other, their limbs fusing and forming an archway above the gate where, in more provident days, many a wagoner must have halted his team while he gathered a capful of the Apple tree's bounty to take home to his wife.

THE WILD CHERRY

*I*n my neighbourhood one does not often see Wild Cherry trees standing in the open, but they are frequently to be found in woodland, and particularly around the edges of woods. Here in East Anglia we are not often blessed with what is considered typical April weather: mild days with bursts of sunshine interrupted by brief, caressing showers. Far more often, April is marked by cutting north and north-easterly winds, sleet and vicious, stabbing rain, and one is led to wonder what signal the tender young leaves have received to encourage them to break out of their warm, enclosing buds; but they do, and none with a more welcome flourish than the Cherry, whose masses of snow-white blossom will appear, sometimes before its leaves, whatever the weather.

Generally, the Cherry blossom coincides with that most magical of moments, when the last storms of winter blow themselves out in an icy fury and suddenly, at the beginning of May, there comes a day which is almost

WILD CHERRY

PRUNUS AVIUM

Fig. 1

Winter twig of Wild Cherry, showing the typical clusters of bright brown pointed buds, often on short stalks.

Fig. 2

Dense colourful clusters of flower buds and young leaves on 17th April.

Fig. 3

The lovely, pure white flowers, with their yellow-anthered stamens and sepals tinged with magenta, together with young leaves on 30th April.

Fig. 4

Leaves, which are green above and grey-green beneath, and long-stalked glossy red cherries on 29th July. Fruits, if not first eaten by birds, later become blackish.

Fig. 5

The autumn colours of Wild Cherry – yellow, orange-red and purplish-brown – are very distinctive.

Wild Cherry (*Prunus avium*).

Fig. 2

Fig. 3

Fig. 1

Fig. 4

Fig. 5

summer: when the sun shines and the rain drops sparkle and all the young green shoots which have been tentatively poking out of their swollen buds become reckless, cast off the protective bud scales, and seem to grow and expand before one's eyes.

For me, one of the most joyful occasions in the whole farming year was the day when the cattle, that had been yarded or outwintered on one of the parks, were turned onto new, fresh grass. We had a herd of suckler cows, which calved down outside from autumn onwards, and by the end of April their field was poached and muddy and covered with the trodden-in debris of the hay and barley-straw that they had been fed through the winter. For the last month or so, they would have been getting more and more restless, threatening to break out as they smelt the new grass growing in the neighbouring meadows and paddocks. When the great day came, I would go down to the bottom of the park, open the gates wide, and start calling them. It was always an old red-roan Shorthorn cow who responded first, and with her in the lead they came, first at a shambling trot and then at a canter, udders swinging wildly, calves forgotten. The moment they were through the gate, their heads would go down, none of them heeding the querulous mooing of the bewildered calves until they were surfeited with new grass.

In most years they were turned out first onto a big, hilly meadow which was bordered by several different woods. One of these, known as the Big Wood, though only some nine or ten acres in extent, had a lot of Wild Cherry trees, including some of the largest that I have ever seen. Open-grown Cherries, or those at the edges of woods which can spread their branches towards the light, tend to be of moderate height and have a spreading habit, but these, being surrounded by Oaks and Elms, had towered up on tall, almost branchless, stems and displayed their narrow crowns of blossom nearly a hundred feet above the woodland floor. Their trunks were rough, with thick segments of bark splitting along the lines of the horizontal lenticels and curling outwards from the tree, and some of the lower branches in their crowns were reflexed downwards at an acute angle. Another very big Cherry tree, probably of the same age, grew at the top edge of the wood, where the lane ran through, dividing it from the Chestnut coppice opposite. This one had grown sideways rather than upwards, several of its large branches arched across the lane, so that after flowering a drift of snowy blossoms lay across the road. One of the branches carried a huge 'Witch's Broom'.

THE HOLLY

*I*t is hard to dissociate the Holly from the Christmas season. Families plan expeditions to particular trees, well known for their berry-bearing propensities, and come back laden with Holly branches adorned with clusters of bright scarlet berries. Hollies bear their male and female flowers on different trees, which is why some trees regularly bear good crops of berries while others – the male trees – never bear fruit. In some years, however, when there has been a spell of hard weather before Christmas, the Holly gatherers may be disappointed, arriving at their favourite tree only to find that Fieldfares and Blackbirds have been there before them, and stripped the tree of all its fruit.

Being evergreen, the Hollies stand out more in winter, and there is no denying the attractiveness of the typical Christmas card concept of glossy dark green Holly leaves and red berries against a snowy background. It is worth remembering, however, that 'The Holly bears a blossom, as white as lily-flower'. As with most trees, the amount of Holly blossom varies from year to year. I remember one season when it was particularly profuse, and as I walked through an overgrown garden at the top of the lane near my house, where a number of large, old Holly trees grew, its subtle fragrance was quite noticeable. This old garden had been derelict for several years since the seventeenth-century cottage which had stood there had, sadly, been pulled down. The cottage, like many in remote situations, had been the gamekeeper's, and the garden was full of old-fashioned perennials such as Michaelmas Daisies and Hollyhocks; there was a huge bush of Rosemary, a fine Darcy Spice apple tree, a veritable jungle of overgrown soft-fruit bushes and a large Walnut tree which generally yielded a good crop of nuts. Several of the Hollies had grown into fairly large trees, although not so tall as those in a nearby wood, some of which, drawn up by the Oaks and Elms around them, had topped fifty feet.

HOLLY

ILEX AQUIFOLIUM

Fig. 1

Holly shoot with young leaves emerging on 17th May.

Fig. 2

Male and female flowers are borne on separate trees; this drawing shows the female flowers, each of which has four white petals, four abortive stamens and a globular green pistil. They arise in clusters from the leaf axils. Hollies are evergreen, and typical leaves are armed with the familiar sharp spines.

Fig. 3

Male flowers on 19th May. They have four white petals, four stamens with yellow anthers, and no pistils, and they are borne in dense bunches. Leaves, particularly in the upper part of the tree where they are less liable to browsing by cattle or deer, may be entire or furnished with only a few spines.

Fig. 4

Shoot with ripe fruit on 9th October. The scarlet berries may persist on the tree through the winter, but in hard weather are soon eaten by birds. Leaves from the previous year, near the base of the twig, have faded and will soon fall.

Fig. 5

Old leaves fall from the tree throughout the summer, sometimes turning a deep shade of yellow.

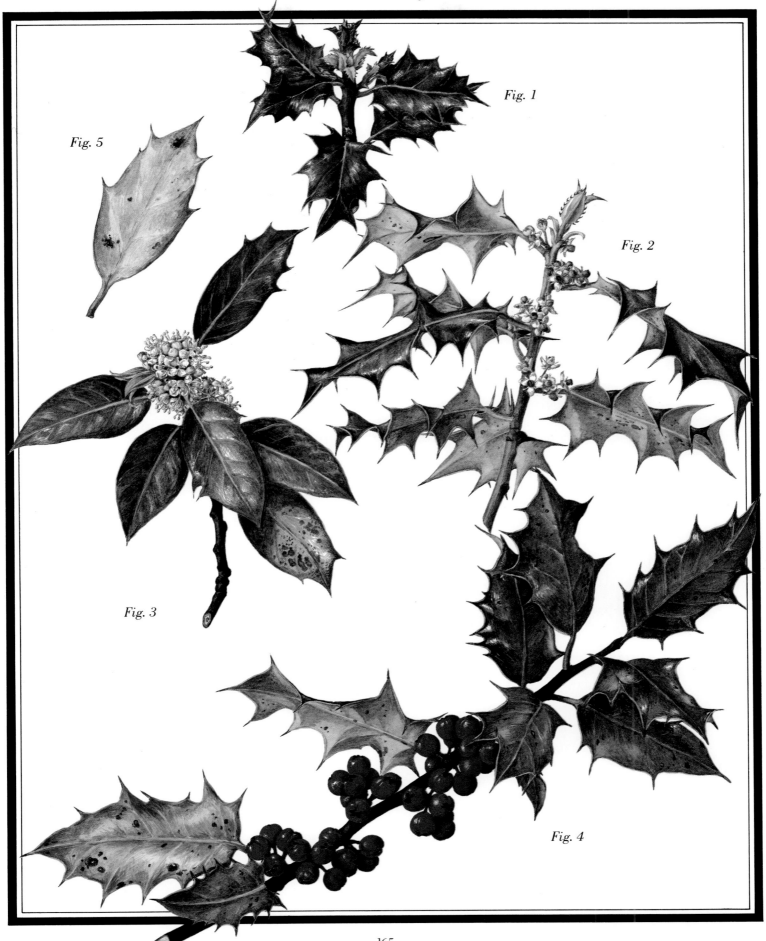

Fig. 1

Fig. 5

Fig. 2

Fig. 3

Fig. 4

THE LOCUST TREE

he Locust Tree was given a boost early in the nineteenth century by William Cobbett, who returned from America full of enthusiasm for its potential as a timber tree, as a result of which many landowners planted it. In the event, its fluted stems proved quite unsuitable for processing in sawmills, but doubtless its brief period of popularity was responsible for the odd trees that one finds today in established woodland.

Near my house is a wood that must have been planted around the 1830s. Some ten years ago it was clear-felled and replanted, except for a fringe of mature trees that were left as a windbreak around the perimeter. They include Elms, Ash, Turkey Oaks, Sycamores, Hornbeams and several other species, but no Locust Trees. Dotted among the Scots Pine and Sycamore that make up the new planting, however, are two or three young *Robinia* which must have arisen as suckers from the root systems of felled trees. On another estate in the neighbourhood, I have come across both mature trees and sucker shoots in woodland, so no doubt the species will remain an occasional constituent of mixed woodland.

As a planted tree in parks and gardens, it is fairly common, and deservedly so, for it is a handsome tree both in summer and winter, and its drooping racemes of white flowers, fragrant and typical of the Leguminosae or Pea family, are particularly attractive.

THE BOX AND THE STRAWBERRY TREE

hese are two little evergreen trees, both of them indigenous in the British Isles, but of very localised occurrence.

The singularity of finding Box growing as a wild tree is emphasised by the fact that several places have been named after it. These include Boxley on the North Downs, where it was seen by John Aubrey, the seventeenth-century antiquary and naturalist who first brought it to the notice of botanists, the Cotswold village of Boxwell and, most famous of all, Box Hill in Surrey. The last is a botanist's paradise, for not only are there pure woods of Beech, Yew and Box, and areas of mixed woodland, but also chalk scrub and chalk grassland, ensuring a varied and fascinating flora throughout the growing season, and including an unusual number of rare or uncommon species.

Elsewhere the Box is only found as a planted tree, occasionally in woodland, more often in gardens where it is often trimmed to form small, neat hedges or topiary figures. So treated, it neither flowers nor fruits, but in gardens, after being well watered at the end of a hot summer's day, it will emit the characteristic subtle fragrance that is only brought out by a combination of heat and humidity.

That smell always reminds me of the gardens of my early youth, when my family lived on the Asiatic shore of the Bosphorus; and it was then, too, that I first made the acquaintance of the Strawberry Tree.

We had a house, for the best part of each summer, on Antigone, one of a group of small islands known as the Prince's Islands, in the Sea of Marmara. In that benign climate the Strawberry Trees ripened their fruits early, and in late summer, before we moved back to the mainland, they would already be a wonderful deep scarlet. This intense colour, as if they were lit by an inner fire, together with their rough texture and satisfyingly spherical form, ensured them a place, together with such things as Swallowtail Butterflies, Praying Mantises and Trap-door Spiders, among my enduring childhood memories.

When I next came upon a Strawberry Tree, it was many years later, in the rather overgrown garden of an Elizabethan manor house in Suffolk. At first glance I took it for a Holm Oak, but then I noticed a hanging fruit, glowing like a glass bauble on a Christmas Tree, and recognised it instantly as an old friend.

One day I hope that I will have the good fortune to see the *Arbutus* growing, as the old song has it:

> '*By the borders of Leane,*
> *So slender and shapely*
> *In her girdle of green;*'

for it is only there, in the woods around Lough Leane near Killarney, and in a very few other localities in western Ireland, that the Strawberry Tree grows wild in the British Isles.

LOCUST TREE

ROBINIA PSEUDOACACIA

Fig. 1

The winter twig of the Locust Tree is reddish-brown, with very small scaleless buds set in a spiral, each one protected by a pair of short spines. Until the leaves fall, the buds are completely concealed by the bases of the leaf stalks.

Fig. 2

Young leaves emerging on 15th May. This example is from a sucker shoot, and has well-developed spines.

Fig. 3

Flowering shoot at the end of June. The white pea-type flowers hang down in long racemes. The leaves are pinnate with opposite pairs of stalked, oval, entire leaflets.

Fig. 4

Seed pods on 21st August.

Fig. 5

Ripe seed pods on 4th October.

Fig. 6

Pale yellow autumn leaf in early October.

Locust Tree (*Robinia pseudoacacia*).

Fig. 1

Fig. 3

Fig. 2

Fig. 4

Fig. 5

Fig. 6

BOX

BUXUS SEMPERVIRENS

Fig.1

The Box is an evergreen and is thickly clothed with very small, dark green, shiny, stiff, ovate leaves. They are borne in opposite pairs on short stalks, have whitish midribs and entire margins, and emit a sweet scent, particularly in warm and humid conditions. This figure shows a flowering twig on 8th April. The flower clusters grow from the leaf axils and consist of up to half a dozen male flowers, each of which has four stamens with bright yellow anthers. Here and there, a female flower can be seen poking out from among the male flowers; three bluish-green styles topped by yellowish stigmas.

Fig.2

Twig bearing fruits on 4th September. The fruits are blue-green capsules topped by three little horns. These have already started to turn brown. Later, they will split into three valves (left) releasing small, hard, shiny-black seeds. In the leaf axils of the young shoots can be seen the whitish buds of next year's flowers.

Fig. 1

Fig. 2

STRAWBERRY TREE

ARBUTUS UNEDO

Fig. 1

The Strawberry Tree is an evergreen, a member of the Heath family, and has the peculiarity of flowering and fruiting at the same time, in October.

The twigs are dark in colour, rough and, especially towards their extremities, hairy; the buds very small and inconspicuous.

The leaves are narrowly ovate, or obovate, and finely toothed. They are dark green and shiny above, paler below with a whitish midrib, and glabrous.

The flowers are bell-shaped, reminiscent of the flowers of Cross-leaved Heath or Bearberry, and hang down from the extremities of the twigs in loose panicles. They are greenish-white in colour, more or less tinged with pink, and fragrant. Within each flower is a globular green ovary surmounted by an erect style and surrounded by ten stamens with crimson anthers.

The fruit is a round berry with a granular surface, resembling a ripe strawberry. It takes a year to ripen, progressing from white through green and yellow to scarlet, and finally a splendid deep crimson. Birds are fond of these fruits and help to scatter the small hard seeds which are contained in their cores.

Fig. 1

SYNOPSIS OF SPECIES

FAMILY FAGACEAE
Beech
Fagus sylvatica L.
Origin: native.
Distribution: native on chalks and limestones of southern England. As planted tree throughout area.
Habitat: woods, hedgerows, downlands; any reasonably fertile soils.

Pedunculate or Common Oak
Quercus robur L.; syn. *Q. pedunculata* Ehrh.
Origin: native.
Distribution: widespread throughout area.
Habitat: woods and hedgerows in lowland areas, especially on clays and heavy loams.

Sessile or Durmast Oak
Quercus petraea (Matt.) Liebl.; *Q. sessiliflora* Salisb.
Origin: native.
Distribution: tends to replace *Q. robur* in parts of Wales, north-western England and Scottish highlands. Occasional elsewhere. Hybrids occur between *Q. petraea* and *Q. robur*.
Habitat: prefers lighter, drier and shallower soils than *Q. robur*, and is more at home in hilly and even mountainous areas.

Turkey or Moss-cup Oak
Quercus cerris L.
Origin: introduced from eastern Mediterranean region in seventeenth century; naturalised in south.
Distribution: throughout most of area, commonest in south, increasing.
Habitat: woods, hedgerows etc., on most soils.

Holm or Evergreen Oak
Quercus ilex L.
Origin: introduced from Mediterranean region in early sixteenth century.
Distribution: sporadic as planted tree throughout most of area; commonest around south coast of England and Wales.
Habitat: mostly as planted tree in mixed woodland; often found near the sea; occasionally naturalised.

Sweet or Spanish Chestnut
Castanea sativa Mill.
Origin: introduced, probably by Romans.
Distribution: thoroughly naturalised in southern parts of British Isles, otherwise only as planted tree, decreasing northwards.
Habitat: mainly woods, preferring light soils.

FAMILY BETULACEAE
Silver or Warty Birch
Betula pendula Roth.; syn. *B. verrucosa* Ehrh; *B. alba* L.
Origin: native.
Distribution: widespread throughout area.
Habitat: in mixed or pure Birch woodland and on heaths, moors, hills and mountains up to 2,500 ft. Prefers lighter soils such as sands, peats and gravels.

Hairy, Downy or Brown Birch
Betula pubescens Ehrh.
Origin: native.
Distribution: widespread.
Habitat: replaces *B. pendula* in damper situations, otherwise similar.

Alder
Alnus glutinosa (L.) Gaertn.
Origin: native.
Distribution: throughout area.
Habitat: beside rivers and streams, lakes and ponds and on swampy ground where it sometimes forms small woods or 'carrs'.

Hornbeam
Carpinus betulus L.
Origin: native.
Distribution: native in south-eastern England, and in a few isolated spots westwards to south Wales, otherwise planted.
Habitat: mainly in mixed woodland and in hedgerows.

Hazel
Corylus avellana L.
Origin: native.
Distribution: common throughout area.
Habitat: chiefly found as coppice underwood and as a component of hedgerows.

FAMILY SALICACEAE
White Willow
Salix alba L.
Origin: native.
Distribution: throughout area except extreme north.
Habitat: by rivers, streams, lakes and ditches.

Crack Willow
Salix fragilis L.
Origin: native.
Distribution: native south of the Scottish Highlands; as planted tree farther north and in Ireland.
Habitat: similar to *S. alba*, often growing together.

Goat Willow or Great Sallow
Salix caprea L.
Origin: native.
Distribution: widespread throughout area.
Habitat: woodlands, hedges and thickets; on damp and dry sites.

Black Poplar
Populus nigra L.
Origin: native.
Distribution: now very uncommon as a wild tree but still found in East Anglia, the Midlands and Welsh borders.
Habitat: as hedgerow or woodland tree on alluvial soils of fens and river valleys.

Black Italian Poplar
Populus 'Serotina'; syn. *P.* x *canadensis* Moench var. *serotina* (Hartig.) Rehd.
Origin: arose in the mid-eighteenth century as the result of a crossing between *P. nigra* and an American species *P. deltoides*.
Distribution: widespread as a planted tree.
Habitat: plantations, roadsides, riversides, occasionally in woodland.

Aspen
Populus tremula L.
Origin: native.
Distribution: fairly general throughout the area; very common in Scotland and Ireland; least common in south-eastern England.
Habitat: damp woods, hillsides, heaths; occasionally in hedgerows.

White Poplar or Abele
Populus alba L.
Origin: doubtfully native, possibly a very early introduction.
Distribution: grows most naturally in south-eastern England, planted elsewhere.
Habitat: roadsides, hedgerows, riversides, etc., often forming thickets or sucker shoots.

Grey Poplar
Populus canescens (Ait.) Sm.
Origin: probably native.
Distribution: widely planted over much of area, but only growing as a wild tree in the south.
Habitat: beside rivers and streams and in damp woods.

Balsam Poplar, Balm of Gilead
Populus gileadensis Rouleau.
Origin: introduced from North America.
Distribution: uncertain, since there are several different species and cultivars that are widely planted, and their nomenclature is very confused.
Habitat: roadsides, riversides, woods.

FAMILY JUGLANDACEAE
Walnut
Juglans regia L.
Origin: introduced, probably by the Romans.
Distribution: common in south, less so northwards to Scotland.
Habitat: as bird-sown tree in hedgerows, alongside old railway lines, etc.

FAMILY ULMACEAE
English Elm
Ulmus procera Salisb.; syn *U. campestris* L.
Origin: native and unique to England.
Distribution: the predominant species of Elm throughout the Midlands and much of southern England.
Habitat: hedgerows in fertile agricultural land. Seeds are sterile, but it suckers freely.

Smooth-leaved Elm
Ulmus carpinifolia Gleditsch.; syn. *U. nitens* Moench.
Origin: possibly native or a very early introduction.
Distribution: replaces *U. procera* in much of East Anglia and in east Kent. The Cornish Elm, *U. carpinifolia* var. *cornubiensis* (syn. *U. stricta*.) is a variety, and replaces *U. procera* in Cornwall and west Devon.
Habitat: similar to that of *U. procera*, but more commonly found also as a woodland tree.

Wych Elm or Scotch Elm
Ulmus glabra Huds.; syn. *U. montana* Stokes.
Origin: native.
Distribution: common, but at a low density in southern England, increasing northwards; the commonest Elm in Scotland.
Habitat: woodland or hedgerow tree in south, in the north also in upland glens and beside rivers and streams. Unlike other Elms, it does not sucker, but seeds readily.

Dutch Elm
Ulmus x *hollandica* Mill.; syn. *Ulmus major* Sm.
Origin: hybrid between *U. glabra* and *U. carpinifolia*, probably introduced in seventeenth century.
Distribution: sporadic in South and Midlands.
Habitat: parkland and hedgerows.

FAMILY ACERACEAE
Field Maple
Acer campestre L.
Origin: native.
Distribution: common in South and Midlands except on acid soils; not native in Scotland, probably native but scarce in Ireland.
Habitat: hedgerows and the edges of woods and as a component of hedges on lime-rich soils.

Sycamore or Great Maple ('Plane' in Scotland)
Acer pseudoplatanus L.
Origin: introduced, either by Romans or in early Middle Ages.
Distribution: thoroughly naturalised and widespread throughout area.
Habitat: very varied – woods, hedgerows, thickets – any site where its seedlings are allowed to grow.

Norway Maple
Acer platanoides L.
Origin: introduced in seventeenth century.
Distribution: Common in south, becoming less so northwards.
Habitat: uncommon outside of amenity plantings, but occasional in woods and hedgerows.

FAMILY TILIACEAE
Common Lime
Tilia x *europaea* L.; syn. *T. vulgaris* Hayne.
Origin: natural hybrid between *T. platyphyllos* and *T. cordata*; possibly native.
Distribution: widespread as a planted tree.
Habitat: much planted in churchyards and avenues; occasional in woodland and on roadsides.

Large-leaved Lime
Tilia platyphyllos Scop.; syn. *T. grandifolia* Ehrh.
Origin: native.
Distribution: as a wild tree only in the Wye valley, a few woods in south Yorkshire and near Morecambe Bay in Lancashire.
Habitat: limestone woods and cliffs.

Small-leaved Lime
Tilia cordata Mill.; syn. *T. parvifolia* Ehrh.
Origin: native.
Distribution: localised, mainly on limestone soils, in England and Wales.
Habitat: in woods on basic soils and on limestone cliffs.

FAMILY OLEACEAE
Ash
Fraxinus excelsio L.
Origin: native.
Distribution: abundant on suitable

soils throughout most of the area, replacing Beech as the typical tree of limestone soils from the Derbyshire Dales northwards.
Habitat: woods, hedgerows, etc., preferring a rich, moist, alkaline soil.

FAMILY PLATANACEAE
London Plane
Platanus x *acerifolia* (Ait.) Willd.
Origin: hybrid between Oriental Plane, *P. orientalis* and American Plane, *P. occidentalis*, which arose in Europe about 1750 and was introduced to Britain soon afterwards.
Distribution: common as planted tree in south of area, decreasing northwards to mid Scotland.
Habitat: mainly in towns and cities; in the country seldom encountered outside parks and gardens.

FAMILY HIPPOCASTANACEAE
Horse Chestnut
Aesculus hippocastanum L.
Origin: introduced late sixteenth or early seventeenth century.
Distribution: abundant throughout most of England, less so in Scotland and Ireland.
Habitat: in the countryside on roadsides, village greens, occasionally in woodland.

FAMILY ROSACEAE
Hawthorn, Whitethorn, Quickthorn or May
Crataegus monogyna Jacq.
Origin: native.
Distribution: abundant throughout area.
Habitat: woodlands, thickets, rough meadows and commons, but chiefly as a component of hedges.

Whitebeam
Sorbus aria (L.) Crantz.
Origin: native.
Distribution: native on chalk and limestone soils in southern England and Ireland.
Habitat: in hilly or downland valleys, and in hedgerows on chalk, limestone and sometimes sandy soils.

Rowan or Mountain Ash
Sorbus aucuparia L.
Origin: native.
Distribution: throughout area, commoner in upland districts.
Habitat: hilly country (to elevations of well over 2,000 ft. in Scotland); often around crofts and beside highland streams. Elsewhere occasional in woodland, heathland, etc.

Wild Service Tree
Sorbus torminalis (L.) Crantz.
Origin: native.

Distribution: sporadic in southern England and Wales; most frequent in south-east.
Habitat: generally isolated trees in old woodland.

Crab Apple
Malus sylvestris Mill.; syn. *M. pumila* Mill.; *Pyrus malus* L.
Origin: native.
Distribution: scattered throughout area, south of Scottish Highlands.
Habitat: hedgerows and woodland.

Wild Cherry or Gean
Prunus avium L.
Origin: native.
Distribution: widespread throughout most of area, north to Scottish border.
Habitat: mainly woodland, sometimes in hedgerows.

FAMILY AQUIFOLIACEAE
Holly
Ilex aquifolium L.
Origin: native.
Distribution: widespread throughout area.
Habitat: very varied: woodlands, hedgerows, scrubland, upland glens, etc.

FAMILY LEGUMINOSAE
Locust Tree or False Acacia
Robinia pseudoacacia L.
Origin: introduced in seventeenth century.
Distribution: scattered, mainly in South and Midlands.
Habitat: apart from amenity planting, it is mainly found in woodland, as a survivor from the days when it was thought to have potential as a timber tree.

FAMILY BUXACEAE
Box
Buxus sempervirens L.
Origin: native.
Distribution: as a wild tree only on chalk or limestone soils in a few places in Kent, Surrey, Buckinghamshire and Gloucestershire. Elsewhere much planted.
Habitat: typically in mixed woodland on chalk hills with Beech, Yew, Oak, etc., sometimes in pure stands.

FAMILY ERICACEAE
Strawberry Tree
Arbutus unedo L.
Origin: native.
Distribution: native only in Ireland, chiefly in neighbourhoods of Killarney and Sligo.
Habitat: in woods on limestone soils around lakes in Ireland. Elsewhere uncommonly as planted tree.

Balsam Poplar (*Populus gileadensis*).

GLOSSARY

ABORTIVE: (of the parts of a flower, e.g. the stamens); imperfect, stunted (see also RUDIMENTARY).

ALTERNATE: (of the arrangement of buds on a twig); set alternately, but on the same plane.

ANTHER: The organ at the tip of the stamen which is divided into two cells containing pollen.

APEX: the end of a leaf, seed or other organ farthest away from the stem; the tip, (see also BASE).

APPRESSED: (of a bud); lying flat against the stem.

AURICLE: ear-like lobe at the base of a leaf.

AXIL: the angle between leaf vein and midrib or between leaf stalk and stem.

BASE: the end of a leaf, seed or other organ nearest to the stem; the end of a twig nearest to the branch from which it springs (see also APEX).

BRACT: leaf-like organ at the base of the flower – where present, there may be one or many, and though very variable, they differ from the stem leaves in structure and are generally smaller.

BROWSE: (of cattle, deer, etc.); to feed on the lower leaves and twigs of trees.

CALYX: the outer whorl of a flower, consisting of sepals.

CAMBIUM: a layer of tissue situated under the inner bark (phloem) of a tree, which is responsible for forming the annual rings.

CANOPY: the upper layer of a forest formed by the crowns of the trees.

CATKIN: a very simple form of the spike, generally but not necessarily pendulous, in which clusters of small, sessile flowers are borne on an undivided stalk.

CLONE: any one of a group of plants grown vegetatively (i.e. by cuttings, grafting, etc., or from a sucker shoot) and deriving from a single parent.

COMPOUND: (of a leaf); composed of a number of leaflets.

COPPICE: to cut back trees to ground level so that they may shoot again; or an area of woodland managed in this way for the production of poles.

COROLLA: the inner whorl of a flower, consisting of petals.

CORYMB: a form of inflorescence in which the flower stalks arise successively (as opposed to an umbel where they all arise from the same point) but with the flowers borne more or less on the same plane as a result of the outer stalks being longer than the inner ones.

CROWN: (of a tree); the upper branches, twigs and foliage.

CULTIVAR: cultivated variety of (usually) a clone.

ENTIRE: (of a leaf); with simple margin, lacking teeth.

EPICORMIC SHOOTS: shoots which arise at need from dormant buds located under the tree bark.

FILAMENT: (as a part of a flower); the stalk of a stamen, bearing the anther at its tip.

GLABROUS: hairless, smooth.

GLANDULAR: (of hairs or bristles); terminating in a minute swelling or droplet.

GLAUCOUS: blue-green or whitish, as in the bloom on a plum.

HANGER: a wood on an escarpment or steep hillside.

HERMAPHRODITE: (of a flower); having both stamens and pistil.

HONEYDEW: sugary material secreted by aphids.

IMBRICATED: overlapping, like fish scales or tiles.

INFLORESCENCE: cluster of flowers, flower-head.

LAMMAS SHOOTS: the secondary growth of leafy shoots, typical of the Oaks but also occurring in other species, which takes place after midsummer. Lammas Day is the first of August.

LANCEOLATE: (of leaves); shaped like the blade of a lance; a long narrow oval, broadest near the base and tapering towards the pointed apex.

LAYER: (in hedge-laying); a stem that has been partially cut through and lowered into position.

LEAF SCAR: a usually crescent-shaped scar around a bud, marking the point of attachment of the stalk of a fallen leaf.

LENTICEL: a breathing pore on a shoot or branch, or on the trunk of a tree.

LOBE: the rounded projections formed by indentations in the margin of a leaf.

MAST: the fallen fruits of forest trees, in particular Beech and Oak.

MEALY: (of e.g. a leaf); characterised by very short hairs which have the appearance of meal and can easily be rubbed off with a finger.

NODE: the point on a branch or twig where a bud or shoot arises, often marked by a change in the direction of growth.

OBOVATE: (of a leaf); ovate, becoming broader towards the apex.

OBOVOID: ovoid, becoming broader towards the apex.

OVARY: the enlarged base of the pistil, containing the seed germs, from which the fruit develops.

OVATE: (of a leaf); egg-shaped in outline, broader towards the base.

OVOID: solid, egg-shaped body, broader towards the base.

PALMATE: (of a leaf); shaped like the palm of a hand, with long, radiating lobes.

PANICLE: an inflorescence whose axis is divided into branches which may branch again and which bear numerous flowers.

PEDUNCLE: flower or fruit stalk.

PETAL: one of the divisions of the corolla.

PETIOLE: leaf stalk.

PINNATE: (of a leaf); having a succession of leaflets on either side of the midrib.

PISTIL: the female part of a flower comprising the ovary, style and stigma. POLLARD: to cut back a tree to within about six feet of ground level, so that it may shoot again; or a tree that has been treated in this manner.

POME: a succulent fruit, such as an apple, having its seeds grouped at the centre.

PRODUCED: extended, continued.

PUBESCENT: covered with downy hairs.

RACEME: an inflorescence whose flowers are borne on stalks arising from an undivided axis.

REFLEXED: turned back, recurved.

RHIZOMORPH: a root-like process, e.g. the hyphae or subterranean filaments which form the basic structure of a fungus, and from which the fruiting bodies arise.

RUDIMENTARY: (of the parts of a flower, e.g. the stamens); very stunted, barely perceptible (see also ABORTIVE).

SAMARA: a membranous wing attached to a seed capsule and designed to assist its passage through the air.

SEPAL: one of the divisions (intermediate between a leaf or bract and a petal) of the calyx.

SERRATE: resembling the teeth of a saw. SESSILE: stalkless.

SINUATE: having a wavy margin.

SPIKE: an inflorescence whose flowers are sessile on an undivided axis.

SPIRALLY: (of the arrangement of buds on a twig); set in a spiral or more or less random fashion.

SPUR: a short, woody shoot bearing, or having formerly borne, flowers or leaves; especially on fruit trees.

STAMEN: the male organ of a flower, several of which are usually grouped around the pistil, with the pollen-bearing anther at its tip.

STIGMA: the terminal organ of the pistil which receives the pollen.

STIPULE: small, narrow, leaf-like appendages sometimes found at the base of leaf or petiole or at stem nodes.

STOOL: base of stump of a coppiced tree.

STYLE: the part of the pistil (not always present) between the ovary and the stigma.

SUB: almost; e.g. sub-sessile – having a very short stalk.

SUCKER: sapling arising from the roots of an older tree.

VALVE: any one of the sections into which a ripe fruit capsule splits.

WART: woody protuberance, often minute, on a twig.

Pedunculate Oak (*Quercus robur*).
Endpapers. Wild Service Tree (*Sorbus torminalis*).